Cleveland Food Memories

A Nostalgic Look Back at the
Food We Loved, the Places We Bought It,
and the People Who Made It Special

Gail Ghetia Bellamy

GRAY & COMPANY, PUBLISHERS
CLEVELAND

To my mother, Janice Ghetia Orr, who somehow always
finds room for one more at the table.

Gray & Company, Publishers
1588 E. 40th St.
Cleveland, OH 44103

Library of Congress Cataloging-in-Publication Data
Bellamy, Gail Ghetia.
Cleveland food memories / by Gail Ghetia Bellamy.
p. cm.
1. Gastronomy. 2. Food habits—Ohio—Cleveland. I. Title.
TX633.B44 2003
641.'10'30977132—dc22   2003023233
ISBN 1-886228-79-5

Printed in the United States of America
First Printing

Contents

Foreword: A Tour of Our Culinary Past 4

Welcome to "Northeat Ohio" 5

Dining Out

    Dining by the Decades 9

    Cleveland's Favorite Restaurants 14

    Eatertainment 23

    Counter Culture 26

    Department Store Dining 40

    Steaks of the Past: Big on Beef 43

    Have Fork, Will Travel 44

    Hot Food Comin' Through: Working in Restaurants 50

Shopping

    Bringing It All Back Home: Retail Details 59

    Deals on Wheels: Foods Delivered to the Door 64

    The Sweet Stuff 69

    Bread Alone 82

    Made in Cleveland 86

Cooking and Eating at Home

    Through the Kitchen Door 95

    Chilling Out and Heating Up 101

    Food and Fellowship 104

Taste Yesterday Today: A Blast from Our Culinary Past 106

Acknowledgments 110

Sources 111

Photo Credits 112

Foreword: A Tour of Our Culinary Past

This is a book of nostalgia, which, of course, is defined as a longing for something that's no longer around. In putting it together, I laughed, I cried, and I got really hungry.

In the 1930s, Cleveland was home to more than 1,000 restaurants. By 1994, that number had shot up to 20,000, and we're not even including local food retailers and manufacturers. It should go without saying, then, that you aren't going to find every Cleveland restaurant or food store of yesteryear included here. If your favorite spot doesn't appear, it might be because it's still around—Cleveland has lots of food retailers with staying power, and gobs of long-lived restaurants. A few of those are even noted on the following pages by people whose lives they have touched.

So, consider this a whirlwind tour of Cleveland's culinary past rather than a digest of every great restaurant, food store, and locally made food product. Our history is far too fine and flavorful, and our talented cooks and chefs are far too plentiful, to fit into one book. Sit back, smack your lips, lick your chops, and pat your belly as you take a romp through these pages of our collective culinary memories.

Welcome to "North*eat* Ohio"

Imagine that it's a thousand years from now and archaeologists are sifting through the Beatles layer of civilization, looking for the Sinatra layer.

When they get down to city chicken skewers and empty Hough Bakery boxes alongside half-burned little candles, they'll know they've found Twentieth-Century Cleveland. We're a legendary knife-and-fork city, filled with people who can be identified by their food preferences.

You know you're a Clevelander if you're familiar with city chicken. It isn't a bird you ever studied in zoology class or a definition you'll find in most culinary dictionaries, but you can still see the cubed pork and veal in our supermarket butcher cases, sold in packages with those little wooden skewers. If you've ever blown out the candles on a Hough Bakery birthday cake, wiped away an ice-cream moustache after drinking a malted at the Frosty Bar in Higbee's basement downtown, ordered another hot dog at a ball game because you liked the mustard, or eaten way too many candy kisses at Euclid Beach Park, chances are you're a baby boomer who grew up in Cleveland.

Let's face it: The region surrounding Cleveland might just as aptly be called North*eat* Ohio. We love to chow down. Rib fans congregate around smoking grills in the city's parks, lake perch aficionados know where to find a great fish fry, and steak-lovers have their choice of hot spots. We've always had lots of great stuff on our plates, and it's a good thing, too, because we take food seriously.

The Great Seal of the State of Ohio features a sheaf of wheat that symbolizes our agricultural strength. The flag of Cleveland might just as well depict a napkin being tucked into a shirt collar, symbolizing our great chow-houndery. During the warm-weather months, we'll drive way across town for the fare at ethnic fairs and cultural festivals. We talk about food, we read about food, and we reminisce about it.

Maybe you've studied Cleveland's weather and its topography. If so, you know we've got it made for growing some yummy seasonal and regional foods. This is a great area for fruits and vegetables. In summer, we have our pick of robust ears of sweet corn, plump flavorful tomatoes, or juicy peaches. During the autumn harvest season, we have a wealth of opportunities to buy pumpkins and apples. Late winter and early spring bring maple syrup season.

Gardeners and gourmands alike are sometimes surprised to learn that this is also a city of great food products. Cleveland gave the rest of the country Stouffer's Frozen Foods, Chef Boyardee spaghetti sauce, Life Savers candy, and Beeman's Pepsin Gum. But we've kept for ourselves the treasured memories of our favorite food spots. Whenever anybody mentions Euclid Beach frozen custard or Ball Park Mustard within earshot of a couple of Clevelanders, you're bound to hear a sigh of nostalgia.

In fact, we're pretty spoiled. While the rest of the country was probably getting all excited back in 1903 just because ice-cream cones finally arrived on the scene, here in Cleveland we had double cause for celebration: That was also the year Hough Bakery was born. We got to have our cake, and ice-cream cones, too.

We all know how lucky we are. Unlike New Yorkers, we don't have to take a taxi to some dingy downtown grocery store with a produce section the size of an open suitcase just to meet up with an ear of corn—corn that's probably bounced around in the back of a hot truck for a few days, at that. In the fall, we can drive a short distance and buy ripe grapes fresh from the vine. We don't have to wait until they're doctored up and turned into wine, the way those folks do in Napa Valley, California.

On the other hand, if we don't feel like muddying our boots hiking out to pick our own sweet corn or strawberries, we can just tool on over to the West Side Market. Here in Cleveland, we're just the right distance between the fields where food grows, and the stores where it's sold fresh.

PLAYING CHICKEN

If you're thinking that "city chicken" is a bird that jaywalks across the road to get to the other side, forget it. Many Clevelanders have memories of eating meat cubes on skewers as they grew up, but you won't find city chicken defined in *The New Food Lover's Companion*. *Webster's New World Dictionary of Culinary Arts* describes it as "veal cubes served on kabobs," although locals more often describe it as pork, or a mixture of pork and veal.

Native Clevelander Carol Lally Metz recalls, "I remember it as veal and pork cubes, sold in grocery stores, with wooden skewers packed inside. My grandmother used to braise it and serve it with pan gravy."

AS SEEN ON TV: a McDonald's poster featured local celebrities (left to right) Franz the Toymaker, Woodrow the Woodsman, Barnaby and Captain Penny. Meanwhile, Ghoulardi's fans flocked to Manners.

In the past, when our mothers made rhubarb crisp, raspberry jam, pumpkin pie, or apple strudel, they were just as likely to have used homegrown fruit as fruit bought at the store. Good bagels are nothing new to us, and we can find great baklava anytime we want it.

And speaking of ethnic specialties, our city's diversity translates to a rich food supply. In some other parts of the country, it's a chore just to find a town where you can buy pizza that comes out of an oven rather than a freezer case. In Cleveland, we argue over which pizza was the best one we ever tasted. And then we start debating about where to buy the best pepperoni and sausage.

We're also legendary hot dog eaters. With 1.1 million hot dogs consumed, Jacobs Field is one of the country's hot dog–eatingest stadiums. Based on an annual survey of major league ballparks, we take second place only to the 1.5 million hot dogs consumed at Dodger Stadium in Los Angeles.

Today, as in the past, our food tastes remain tied to the richness of the land, the bounty of the lake, the diversity of our city's culture, and the imagination of its cooks.

COMPETITIVE COOKING: Gene Carroll (right, foreground) at the Cleveland Press Brides' Pride Cooking Contest is waited on by women wearing Coca-Cola bottle-cap hats.

Dining Out

**Dining just may be Cleveland's
all-time favorite entertainment. As adults, we
accumulate restaurant experiences the
way we collected baseball cards as kids, trading
memories of great meals with our friends.**

While we may have dined out less frequently in the past, that seems only to have heightened our level of observation. When it comes to restaurant nostalgia, we remember not only where we ate, but who we ate with, what we wore, and how we were treated by the staff. Some folks recall a golden era of hospitality, when restaurant dining was a choreographed event in an environment as glitzy as a stage setting. Others remember the sensory bombardment of their favorite teen hangouts, where music blasted from the jukebox as burgers sizzled on the grill. Restaurants weren't just places where we ate. They were places where we created a lifetime of memories.

Dining by the Decades

Since 1970, Americans have increased their restaurant dining dramatically. Back then, people in this country spent a total of $42.8 billion on food and drink in restaurants. In 2003, that figure is projected to reach $426.1 billion. Today, we spend more than 46 percent of every food dollar in restaurants. And we have a lot of places to choose from. As of the 1990s, there were more 800,000 restaurant locations around the country (870,000 is the current estimate in 2003). About 20,000 of them were in Cleveland.

Nationally, Cleveland may not have been known for being on the culinary cutting edge with wildly distinctive cuisine, but we did elevate to an art the serving of wholesome fare, well executed and beautifully presented. In their 1982 book, *Dining In—Cleveland*, authors Michael DeLuca and Stephen Michaelides (then managing editor and chief editor, respectively, of the Cleveland-based national trade magazine *Restaurant Hospitality*) wrote the following: "Today Cleveland finds herself in the midst of a restaurant renaissance that fulfills the needs of its residents and provides a welcome and surprising respite from the well-received yet simple cuisine that had been the city's hallmark for several decades."

Here are some highlights of Cleveland's restaurant past.

EAT STREET: our culinary skyline ran the gamut from cafes to corner grocery stores.

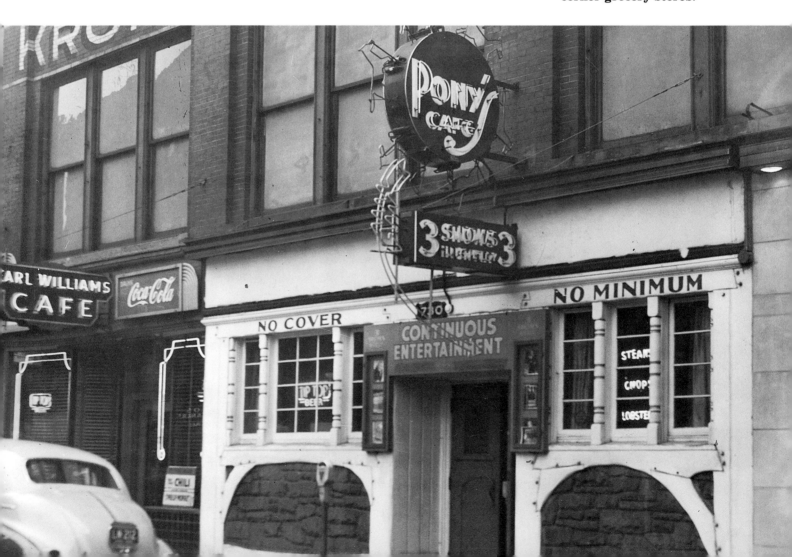

**SELECTED CLEVELAND
RESTAURANT OPENINGS
PRE-1940**

1907: Clark's Restaurant opens
its first outlet on what is now
East Sixth Street

1911: The Colonnade Cafeteria
opens in the Rockefeller
Building

1913: Kornman's opens
on Short Vincent

1918: Guarino's opens
in Little Italy

1920: Rohr's opens
on Chester Avenue

1923: Sokolowski's arrives
on the scene

1924: Stouffer Lunch, the forerunner
of the Stouffer Restaurant
chain, opens

1931: The Silver Grille opens
in Higbee's on Public Square

Chef Boiardi's,
later known as Chef
Hector's, opens at
823 Prospect Avenue

Jim's Steak House
opens on Collision Bend

1932: The English Oak Room
opens in the Terminal Tower

1937: Kiefer's opens at
2519 Detroit Avenue

The Theatrical Grill
opens on Short Vincent

1930s

In the 1930s, Cleveland claimed 120 hotels and 1,073 restaurants. In the 1930s and 1940s, we were a major convention site. In 1937, the Great Lakes Exposition, held on the city's lakefront, promoted the assets of the region. Among the attractions was the Aquacade water ballet and the Horticultural Gardens. And of course, the visitors had to eat. Herman Pirchner's Alpine Village at the Expo seated 600 people and had an automatic rising dance floor that became a stage.

In April 1931, the *American Restaurant Magazine*, a national trade magazine for the restaurant industry, reported on the Cleveland Restaurant Association. Among the city's restaurant movers and shakers were Robert H. Morris of Morris Luncheon; Mrs. Bertha Damon of Damon's Tea Room; W. H. Anders of Anders Cafeteria; Miss Katheryn Carey of the Commodore Coffee Shop; R. D. Clark of Clark's Restaurant Company; Vernon B. Stouffer of Stouffer Corporation; and E. M. Taylor of Mills Restaurant Company.

Later that same year, the magazine carried an article about the opening of the Forum Cafeteria in Cleveland. "Right in the heart of some of the stiffest restaurant competition in the country, they opened last month the seventh unit in their rapidly expanding chain." The cafeteria fed an estimated 4,900 to 5,200 people a day. On the menu were fruit and vegetable salads, celery, olives, tomato juice, sauerkraut juice, fish, roast beef, and baked ham. Standard vegetables were described as "potatoes, beets, stewed tomatoes, corn and kidney beans."

Cafeterias started taking off in the 1920s, thanks to their "what you see is what you get" appeal. But cafeterias and coffee shops weren't our city's only claims to culinary fame. Long before his name summoned images of cake mixes and other food products, Duncan Hines was serving as America's food guide with his *Adventures in Good Eating*. Together with his wife, Hines, a chowhound of renown, kept a journal of places where they ate while traveling, and in 1935 they had a printed version of their list sent to friends in lieu of a Christmas card. On that list were 167 recommended restaurants around the country. By the time the 1955 edition of *Adventures in Good Eating* rolled around, 39 places from the first list had withstood the test of time and remained on the list. Damon's in Cleveland was one of them.

1940s

World War II changed the restaurant dining scene. In 1942, the Office of Price Administration (O.P.A.) issued a maximum price regulation that prevented retailers and wholesalers from charging more than the maximum price they had charged for "cost of living commodities" during the month of March that year. Rationed foods included sugar, coffee, meat (but not fish or game), and processed food (but not fresh vegetables). Eventually, nearly 90 percent of retail food prices were frozen during wartime.

Restaurants prices were also affected. Ceiling prices had to be posted so customers could see them. For example, the menu at Herman Pirchner's Alpine Village at Playhouse Square carried a note that read "All prices listed are our Ceiling Prices or lower than Ceiling Prices. By O.P.A. regulations, our Ceilings are our highest prices from April 4–April 10, 1943. Records of these prices are available for your inspection." Among the items on that menu were Pork Chops, Lake Erie Whitefish, and Calf's Liver, each offered for $1.75.

1950s

Drive-in restaurants were an offshoot of our car culture. They emerged in the 1940s, but really came into their own in the 1950s. Service and speed were the original selling points, but drive-ins also became part of the social scene for young customers who congregated there.

Also, the idea of eat-now-pay-later was catching on. Diner's Club and American Express made it possible to charge your dinner. Fast food began cutting into the market for restaurants that served wholesome American fare, and lunch counters began evolving into coffee shops.

The Smorgasbord in Stow, Ohio, opened by Lillian Jae, was mentioned in the *Duncan Hines' Food Odyssey*, published in 1955. Of Damon's, at 2644 Fairmount and 16712 Shaker Boulevard, Hines wrote, "A good, clean place to eat, with a varied menu." Specifically mentioned was the fact that the restaurant made pastries

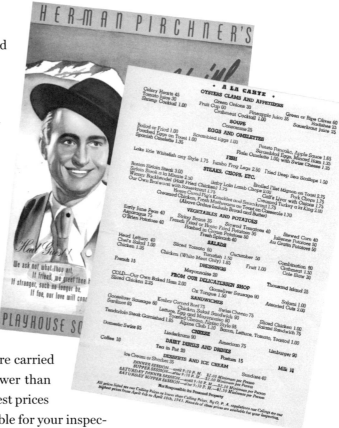

EATERTAINMENT: at Herman Pirchner's Alpine Village, what was on stage was as important as what was on the plate.

FABULOUS FRED: Fred Harvey Restaurant was one of Cleveland's notable spots in the 1950s.

1960s PRICE CHECK

1963: Lunch at Brown Derby Restaurant started at 85 cents. The restaurant locations were Independence, Shaker Heights, and Rocky River Drive in Cleveland.

1968: Howard Johnson's in North Olmsted (24250 Lorain Road) offered fried clam dinners on Fridays for $1.49. The Monday-night chicken fry was the same price.

1968: Otto's Brauhaus, 19126 Detroit Road in Rocky River, had a smorgasbord on Wednesdays, Thursdays, and Fridays, priced at $3 a person.

WHOLE LOTTA SHAKIN': even the salt and pepper shakers had a Polynesian theme at Kon-Tiki in the Sheraton-Cleveland.

and ice cream, plus candy sold at a candy store in the Hotel Cleveland on Public Square. Dinner prices ranged from 85 cents to $1.35.

Among the Cleveland restaurants listed in the 1958 edition of *Adventures in Good Eating* were the Colonnade Cafeterias, Miller's Dining Room, Rohr's, Monaco, Gruber's Restaurant, Tasty Shop Restaurant, the Halle Brothers and Higbee's tearooms, Fred Harvey Restaurant, Kornman's Restaurant, the Tavern Chop House, and the Hickory Grill.

1960s

Although home-style cooking, steak houses, and French food still retained their hold on Cleveland appetites, this was the era when our food tastes started to diversify. Restaurants offering German, Chinese, or Italian food, including pizza, were packing them in. When Hawaii became the 50th state, our interest in Polynesian-style food increased. This was also the era when the number of fast-food restaurants tripled.

1970s

The proliferation of ethnic restaurants continued in the seventies, as did a new interest in Victorian-themed pub-style dining and fern bars. Eventually, the drive-in evolved into the drive-thru, and we were no longer limited to burgers and hot dogs. "I taught at East Tech, and used to go to the Shrimp Boat. One of them was on East 55th. It was a shrimp drive-thru, where they sold French-fried shrimp," recalls Jan DeLucia.

Do-it-yourselfers were happy with the concept of salad bars, and those with an interest in healthful dining embraced Nouvelle Cuisine when it arrived on the scene. Newspaper readers around the country began paying more attention to restaurant critics, too. Here's a list of seventies hot spots in Cleveland, from a 1976 article written by *Plain Dealer* food editor Janet Beighle French ("My 10 Favorite Restaurants"). Note that by this era, ethnic cuisines were here to stay.

Pere Jacques
34105 Chagrin Boulevard
Moreland Hills

Tre Scalini Room
Quagliata's White House
9323 Mentor Avenue, Mentor

Tokyo Garden
21750 Lorain Avenue
Fairview Park

Sam & Jerry's
7503 Granger Road, Valley View

Old Austria
20412 Center Ridge Road
Rocky River

Earth By April
2151 Lee Road
Cleveland Heights

Parthenon, 1518 Euclid Avenue

Middle East Restaurant
1 Carter Manor

Heck's, 2927 Bridge Avenue

Art Museum Cafeteria
Cleveland Museum of Art
11150 East Boulevard

"There's something about food and romance."

Cleveland's Favorite Restaurants

Mmmm. Whether it was Miller's, Mawby's, Manners, or Maharas, the names of some favorite Cleveland restaurants summon memories of specific foods and flavors.

In restaurant lingo, those are known as signature items, and boy, are they distinctive. Mention Mawby's, and the next phrase you're likely to hear is "grilled onions." Mention Miller's, and you'll hear about salads, rolls, and finger bowls. Memories of Manners Big Boy are often accompanied by memories of the Big Boy sauce and strawberry pie. And fans of the long-gone Al Maharas Steak House recall something simply listed on the menu as "That Salad."

Restaurants aren't just places that make meals. They're places where memories are made, where we go to celebrate or to drown our sorrows, places where important things happen like first dates, engagements, and awards dinners. Restaurants are also places of romance.

As native Clevelander Pat Fernberg puts it: "There's something about food and romance. A really good meal is the consummation between science and art, chemistry and ballet, music, and math. That's what makes it such a sensual experience—its textures and colors and sounds. Your senses are engaged the way they are with a really good piece of music."

Speaking of romance, native Clevelander Miriam Carey, author of *52 Romantic Outings in Greater Cleveland*, still carries the torch for a side dish that fell off the menu:

> Most of my siblings and I at one time or another worked at Don's Lighthouse, the charming building at the end of the West Shoreway that features four rounded, copper-topped mini-towers and large arched windows. It was, and still is, legendary. My brother John was the first in our family to work there. Eventually, almost all of us did our time waiting tables or hostessing at the place. Since it was right down the street, Don's was our favorite special-occasion place to go for steaks, and with six kids in tow, this was no small thing for my parents. The ultimate, must-have thing was Don's Dirty Rice, a mixture of rice, onions, and mushrooms that must have hit

MIND YOUR MANNERS: Big Boy sandwiches and strawberry pie at Manners were a mainstay for many Clevelanders.

THE MILLER'S TALE: this Lakewood destination restaurant is most remembered for its "sticky buns," trays of rolls and salads, and home-style cooking.

the grill at some point. It was so moist, mushy, and oily . . . I can still taste it now, and I still wonder who the idiot was that took Don's Dirty Rice off the menu. It's perhaps one of the top five Cleveland Food Crimes of all time, next to the closing of Hough Bakery and the jolting loss of the Silver Grille.

On the following pages, you'll find recollections of some of the city's well-known dining spots. This is just a small sampling of the places that served our favorite fare.

CAPTAIN FRANK'S

For young people, Captain Frank's on the East Ninth Street Pier was a very popular Friday and Saturday night hangout. – *Therese Hummer, Cleveland*

CIRO'S

In 1947, I worked at Ciro's at East 115th and Euclid, while I was still in school. (They also owned a store on 76th and Euclid.) I worked at Pierre's, too; I worked between the two places. Ciro's was lunch food: hamburgers, cheeseburgers, hot dogs, sodas, and milk shakes. At Pierre's, we mostly got the crowd from the Play House. Waffles were a big deal at the time, waffles with ice cream. – *Marge Skof, Cleveland*

NAUTICAL BUT NICE: customers at Captain Frank's Restaurant on the East Ninth Street Pier bought postcards to commemorate their seafood dining experience on the lakefront.

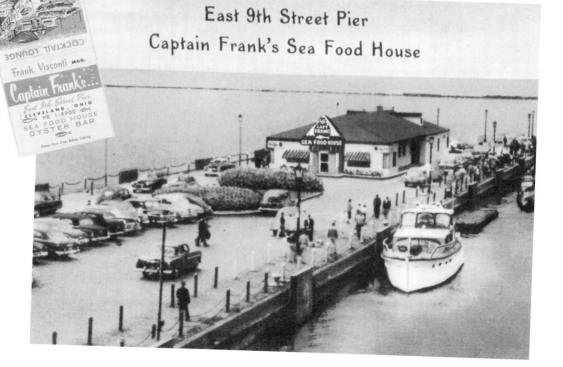

CROSBY'S

One of my earliest food memories was eating out at Crosby's, on East 105th and Carnegie. I was in a bridal party, and it was a wonderful adventure. It was more or less Americanized food, in the 1950s. – *Anna Chenin, Cleveland*

CHEF BOIARDI'S (later Chef Hector's)

"It was very funny to get into; you had to go between buildings to get to it, down in a basement. It was really a wonderful restaurant. The chef was there, and he would come out and talk to the customers. I think I ordered spaghetti and meatballs." – *Anna Chenin*

GIVING MOM A BREAK: in 1951, the Sunday menu at Wade Park Manor featured a chopped sirloin steak family dinner for $2.25 per person.

PASTA PLUS PERSONALITY: in 1964, Chef Hector Boiardi was part of the draw at this Italian restaurant. Today, you might remember him as Chef Boyardee.

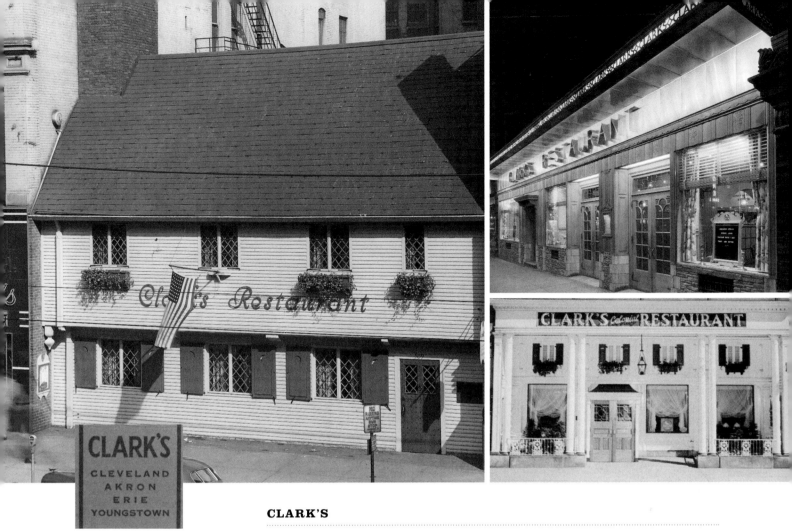

CLARK'S

CLEVELAND
AKRON
ERIE
YOUNGSTOWN

FAMILY FARE: Clark's Restaurants around town provided serious food in a family-friendly environment. Kids who cleaned their plates got to choose a toy to take home, too.

CLARK'S

We used to come to the ball games and would go to Clark's on Shaker Square. We usually ate first, and then went to the ball game. We weren't allowed to buy any of that junk at the ball game. Clark's was the fanciest restaurant I had ever seen. It wasn't all that fancy, really, but we didn't go out much. – *Jan DeLucia, Cleveland*

I remember Clark's Restaurant as a kid. If you cleaned your plate, you could go to the treasure chest where they had trinkets and toys—stuff that seemed like it was worth a million dollars. – *Carl LoPresti, Cleveland*

One of the most popular and successful restaurant chains that I hated to see leave was Clark's. They were great places and, to this day, that's the kind of food I like— meatloaf, pot roast. I used to have breakfast every day at Clark's when I was going to school at Cathedral Latin. I had hotcakes, mostly. They were 35 cents.
– *Sam DeGaetano, Cleveland*

DAMON'S

Over at Fairmount and Cedar, a lot of ladies ate at Damon's. It was the place to go. My husband and I once went there with another couple. The restaurant had red checked tablecloths, and my friend was wearing a red checked blouse. I accused her of wearing a tablecloth for a blouse. I remember it as being a very nice restaurant. – *Pat Bertman Mazoh, Cleveland*

GRUBER'S

Out on Van Aken was the storied Gruber's Restaurant, whose cuisine was elegant and whose maitre d' was tall, white-haired, and imperturbable. The table-hopping was done by Max Gruber himself, and if your table was one that he selected to visit, your social status was immediately enhanced. – *Aaron Jacobson, Cleveland*

When I was young, the elegant restaurant in my neighborhood was Gruber's, where you'd get very fine cuisine. It was where your parents went, but you didn't. – *Lilli Lief, Shaker Heights*

My favorite dessert was the Baked Alaska at Gruber's. – *Karen Perry, Shaker Heights*

HARVEY'S OAK ROOM

My favorite restaurant was Harvey's Oak Room. It was elegant, but it wasn't snooty. The decor was lovely—heavy oak and wood—and the waitresses were uniformed. – *Pat Bertman Mazoh*

HOWARD JOHNSON'S

At the end of the West Shoreway, there was life before Don's Lighthouse.

In the late '50s through the mid-'60s, Howard Johnson's (the original, I always believed) at the entrance to the Shoreway on Cleveland's West Side, was the only spot for the world's best hot dogs on s-q-u-a-r-e toasted buns served in an easy-access, four-sided, slide-out cardboard holder. I thought their logo represented Simple Simon meeting the pie man. – *George Ghetia, Lakewood*

Actually, Howard Johnson opened his first restaurant in Massachusetts in the 1920s. Cleveland didn't get its own Ho-Jo until 1942, when Don Strang, Sr., opened it in the lighthouse building at the end of the Shoreway on the West Side.

However, the idea of wrapping a hot dog in a bun originated right here in the Western Reserve. Around 1900, Harry M. Stevens of Niles, Ohio, first packaged a frankfurter in bread, then upgraded the presentation to a roll. The Howard Johnson chain took that a step further when it offered hot dogs in rectangular buns. In fact, they fancied the presentation in other ways, too, by snipping off the ends of the hot dog, slashing it lengthwise, and cooking it in butter to enrich the flavor.

Although Howard Johnson's started as an ice-cream place, today the lingering memories of our experience are most likely to include orange roofs; weathervanes

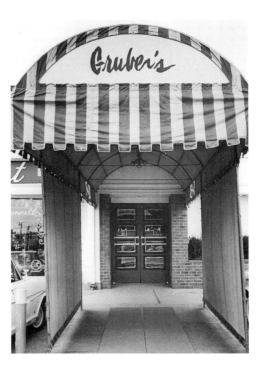

SHADES OF YESTERDAY: an elegant awning set the scene for fine dining at Gruber's in 1958.

HOT AND COLD: Howard Johnson's summons memories of fried clams and ice cream—served under an orange roof.

featuring a chef, a boy, and a dog; unique hot dogs; and platters of fried clams—a menu specialty no doubt inspired by the company's Cape Cod roots. We also might recall Ho-Jo Cola, a Coca-Cola clone served at the restaurants. By the mid-1950s, there were more than 400 Howard Johnson's around the country, many of them along the nation's turnpikes. It became a place we associated with vacation.

MILLER'S DINING ROOM

We went to Miller's Dining Room on rare occasions. The thing that my sister and I remember is that they passed around a huge tray of just-out-of-the-oven rolls, sticky buns, and also a tray of salads . . . We went there because it was one of the few restaurants that didn't serve alcohol. My father didn't like distilled spirits and didn't drink wine because he didn't like the taste. – *Stephen G. Michaelides, Cleveland Heights*

I remember going to Miller's. Chicken à la king in a basket was our all-time family favorite, and all you could eat of the sticky buns, cornbread rolls, and muffins. We left fat and happy. It was festive, with everybody being there together. It gave us an all-around good feeling – *Ellie Yanky, Berea*

The cultural icon that stands out is Miller's Dining Room in Lakewood. This old place, near Woodward Avenue and Detroit, was about as old-fashioned as it got. The monstrous dining room was always filled with older ladies playing cards in the

SIGNATURE STUFF: a piggy bank, demitasse set, and ashtray served as Howard Johnson souvenirs.

LAKEWOOD LANDMARK: for many years, Miller's was known as much for its liquor-free environment as it was for its sticky buns, salads, and finger bowls.

afternoons, and their families would materialize around dinnertime. Linen tablecloths and old-fashioned place settings (all the forks, knives, and even finger bowls were laid out at each place) gave Miller's a formal, at-your-granny's-club air. Large women walked around the dining room carrying oversized trays filled with small salads, and you could take your pick—coleslaw, Jell-O, beets, little salads, and small glasses of tomato juice. I wouldn't be surprised if "aspic" was also an offering, that's how old-fashioned it was. I think you could pick two things from the tray as part of your dinner package. But you kept your eye out for the sticky-bun ladies. They had oversized trays, too, but theirs were stacked with an assortment of breads—big cornbread sticks, dinner rolls, and Miller's signature sticky buns. Warm, mushy, sticky, cinnamon-y, brown sugary, butter-loving sticky buns. You find me a better sticky bun anywhere and I'll be grateful to you forever. For anyone who lived in Lakewood during the reign of Miller's, those memorable sticky buns are the measure against which all other sticky buns must be judged, and though I've searched far and wide, none compare. – *Miriam Carey, Cleveland*

THE STOUFFER'S EXPERIENCE: Stouffer's evolved from a lunch counter to a downtown institution that branched out to the suburbs and offered restaurants ranging from Pete and Charlie's to Top of the Town.

THE NEW YORK SPAGHETTI HOUSE

My husband and I went to the New York Spaghetti House on our first date. We were treated as if we were royalty. It just seemed so romantic. Then, four days later on our second date, he proposed. Which says a lot for the food, and reflects well on the chef. We went there every December 23, the anniversary of our first date. When they closed, it was almost like a personal pain, a palpable ache, because of those memories." – *Pat Fernberg, Cleveland*

MENU MOVES: the distinguished restaurant career of Marie Schreiber (left) ranged from catering for United Airlines to operating Marie Schreiber's Tavern in the Hollenden House Hotel.

SCHNEIDER'S

After our prom, we went to Schneider's on Center Ridge Rd. I graduated from Notre Dame Academy, and a group of us drove over to the West Side, six or eight couples. It was plain food. I think we had steak.
– *Claire A. Wirt, Cleveland*

MARIE SCHREIBER'S

Marie Schreiber operated the food service in the Hollenden Hotel. She was an outstanding operator and had an excellent menu. She was an institution. – *Therese Hummer*

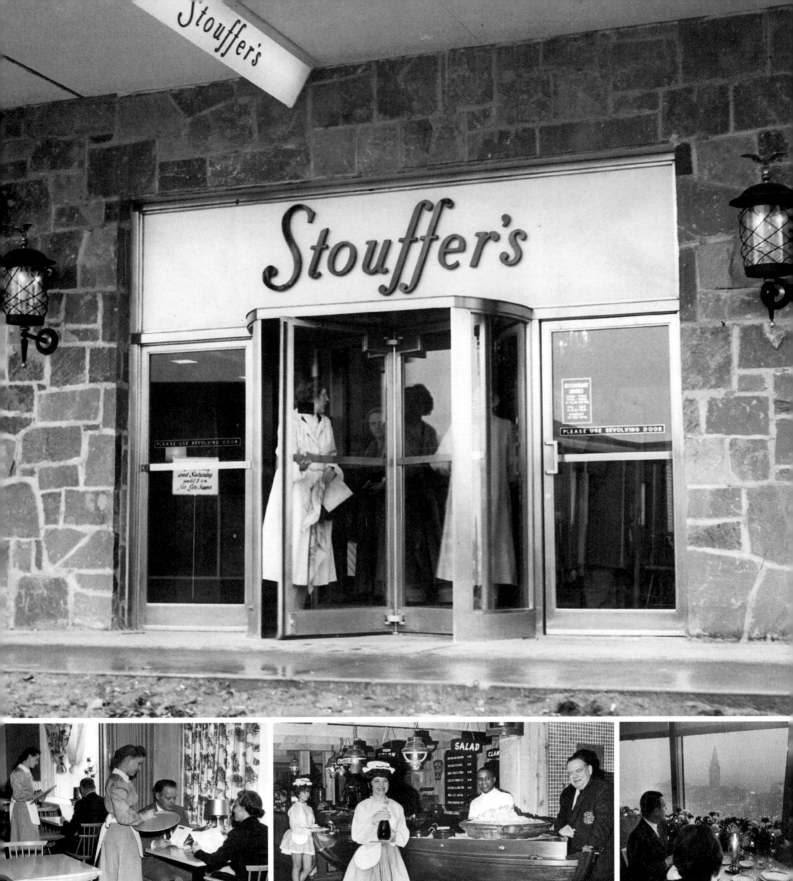

SMORGASBORD IN STOW

We went to the Smorgasbord in Stow for special occasions. I loved eating the apple-sauce as a little kid. I'd go back for seconds on it. – *Susanne Apple, Macedonia*

STOUFFER'S RESTAURANTS

Stouffer's was known for its good food and for the waitresses, who wore conservative uniforms with aprons tied in the back with big bows.

We went to Stouffer's at Shaker Square—very beautiful, elegant, with gold-rimmed mirrors and white linen. – *Sali A. McSherry, Chagrin Falls*

Top of the Town had some very good desserts—especially the black-bottom pie. It had three layers with two kinds of Myers's Rum in it, light and dark. – *Jan DeLucia*

I miss two restaurants—one of them is Stouffer's on Euclid Avenue downtown, right next to Richman Brothers. Stouffer's treated me the way they would have treated my mom, even though I was in my early 20s. And I miss the Apple Walnut Pie Chantilly. I've never been able to find it again, anywhere. I always ate there before ballet class. I still remember the taste of that pie, the fragrance, the perfume of it, and the incredible texture. I haven't been able to re-create it. – *Pat Fernberg*

PLAYING WITH FOOD: carhops, chow, and a pinwheel at Kenny King's . . . What more could a kid want?

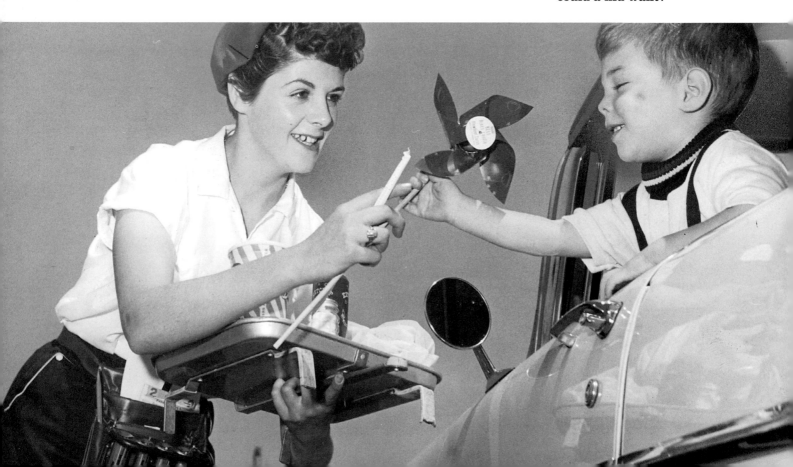

**CLASS IN A GLASS:
Schneider's was a place
for prom dates and more,
with classic cocktails
for adults.**

**KID STUFF: in 1941,
Clark's offered a children's
menu featuring artwork
by Hal Cooper. In later
years, young diners were
invited to join a birthday
club.**

Eatertainment

Many Clevelanders enjoyed the double whammy of making dining out a fun event as well as a filling one. While casual restaurants might have started out as lunch-eonettes and snack bars where workers could grab a quick bite, they evolved into spots where families enjoyed an evening's entertainment for the price of a meal. Long before the legendary New York restaurateur Joe Baum (who opened the Four Seasons in 1959) pioneered the concept of the restaurant as theater, Clevelanders were drawn to some of their favorite eateries by the idea of entertainment.

The phrase "playing with your food" took on new meaning for baby boomers whose parents dined at spots like Manners, where kids could read comic books that brought them up to date on the adventures of Big Boy, Dolly, and Nugget, or at Clark's and Kenny King's, where kids could select a toy out of the treasure chest after cleaning their plates. As Jodi Kanter recalls, "My earliest food memory is when my parents used to take us to Clark's. There were five kids in our family, and if you wanted to go out to eat, that's where you went. All I remember were the toys, a chestful of toys. The food wasn't even the issue."

In case you're wondering what the food was like at the six Clark's restaurants in Cleveland, here's an opinion published in 1955: "Mr. R. D. Clark of Cleveland, who built this group of dining rooms, is one of the Midwest's outstanding restaurateurs," wrote Duncan Hines in *Duncan Hines' Food Odyssey.* Hines called the menu "typically American," citing examples such as beef pot roast, chicken croquettes, and fried scallops, and noting that service was also a specialty at Clark's.

DINNER/DANCE: a stage rose out of the floor and diners beheld the Alpine Village chorus line and well-known vaudeville performers.

"I'd recommend their steaks, fruit gem muffins, oysters, fresh-baked pie, butter pecan ice cream, and the coffee, which is outstanding," he said.

Other customers frequented places that had elaborate forms of entertainment. Herman Pirchner's Alpine Village was known for its entertainment, its colorful owner, and its nightlife.

> I went to nightclubs with my parents because that's what my father [the late Peter Bellamy, entertainment editor of the *Plain Dealer*] did for a living. I loved the Alpine Village. Herman Pirchner pushed the button and the floor rose up and you heard this tremendous grinding. There were always dancing girls, and the floor would bounce. They wore spangled costumes. I ate steak. Herman Pirchner always came over to our table. He was very kind to me, very gentle, and made me feel honored. We were always seated at a table at the right front of the stage, the first or second table in from the corner. From the time I was two, I went there. They didn't have children's portions or doggie bags, and I could never finish my meal, but I loved the food. The Alpine Village was run very tightly. Waiters were Old World, and things were very formal, very exact. The tables were very close together, and Herman Pirchner watched everything. – *Sheila Bellamy, Cleveland Heights*

Stephen G. Michaelides remembers hearing a legendary jazz pianist at the Theatrical Grill. "Because of the blue laws in the city, they wouldn't permit anybody underage to go there during the week because alcohol was served. But on

THEATRICAL-GOERS:
the Theatrical was the
place for drinks, dinner,
and entertainment,
including Duke
Ellington.

Sundays, they would. They had some great jazz people there—Stan Kenton, Gene Krupa, Duke Ellington, and Oscar Peterson. When Oscar Peterson came here, my friends and I all went to the Theatrical Grill and sipped Coke. It was incredible, the thrill of a lifetime."

Clevelander Joe Valencic has two memories that give new meaning to the phrase "dinner dance." He remembers, "I was in Frank Yankovic's Steak House the night Lawrence Welk arrived with his performers in 1972. After dinner, Mr. Champagne Music played the piano and danced. I later read in his autobiography that this was the only time he went out after a show, and he thoroughly enjoyed himself."

But that's not all. Valencic also recalls the following: "I was in the Hofbrau Haus the night the Chicken Dance was introduced to Cleveland in November 1981. The dance looked so ridiculous, no one would try it and the waitresses had to demonstrate it with members of the band and the kitchen staff. By summer, it was a hit."

"There were always dancing girls, and the floor would bounce."

Counter Culture
Casual Meals at Lunch Counters, Burger Joints, Cafeterias, and Diners

In the 1940s, places for casual meals included coffee shops, cafeterias, tearooms, and lunch counters. While those places continued to flourish in Cleveland in the 1950s and 1960s, we also saw burgeoning burger joints and fast-food franchises. Whether you ordered meat loaf, hot dogs, or hamburgers was immaterial: What you ate isn't as important as the memories.

LUNCH COUNTERS

I remember lunch counters in the dimestores—getting chicken salad on toast at the lunch counter at Woolworth's and thinking it was heaven. That was my favorite, forever. It was before they even asked you what kind of bread you wanted toasted; it was just bread. Our parents would give us money—less than a dollar—and I would go there with my girlfriends. For less than a dollar you got your sandwich and something to drink, and could still leave a tip. Woolworth's used to have the WIXY Top 60 hit-record list, and we'd get the list and discuss it at lunch. That was a rite of being a preteen—lunching on your own and discussing records. – *Lyn Byrd, Brunswick*

COUNTER INTELLIGENCE: smart shoppers in the 1960s often sat at the counter for a quick bite at the Woolworth's luncheonette, 306 Euclid Avenue.

"Luncheon counters in Cleveland did not have seating until after World War II. The concept was 'eat and run.'"

When I was a kid, Woolworth's—downtown on the Square by the May Company—had a food counter. I loved their hot dogs and root beer.
– *Tony Macias, Euclid*

We used to eat at Grant's, only at Christmas. That was the only time we were downtown shopping. We'd have meat loaf, mashed potatoes, and corn. We had that all the time. Even after we were grown, my sister and I would still go there and have that to celebrate. They had booth seating. – *Dorothy Bell, Cleveland (Near East Side)*

Mom took you to eat at different places than Dad. My mother preferred the luncheon counters at Kresge's and Woolworth's. She could leave me there with a sandwich and still shop with an eye on me. I think my father took me to the same greasy spoons he went to in the 1920s. We ate at places like the Coney Island next to the Roxy Burlesque, and anonymous lunch counters on East Fourth or Prospect. This was before urban renewal, when East Ninth Street looked like an Edward Hopper painting. Luncheon counters in Cleveland did not have seating until after World War II. The concept was "eat and run." At Kresge's, I would order a club sandwich because it tasted so indescribably delicious. I found out later it was the mayonnaise. We never had mayo at home. – *Joe Valencic, Cleveland (North Collinwood/Beachland)*

DRUG-STORE DEAL: Gray Drug Store downtown served affordable sandwiches, sodas, and more. You could get a grilled steak sandwich for 35 cents.

My friend used to eat at the lunch counter at Kresge's, but my mother would never let me go there. She wouldn't let us eat at any counter. They served french fries and cheeseburgers. You could smell it. – *Helen Weinberger, Cleveland (East 105th and St. Clair)*

A favorite place for me was the Five Cent Coffee House sitting down where the stadium is now. Everything was a nickel—a nickel for a piece of pie. But you would end up paying a quarter for your food. We walked downtown so we could stop there and eat. It cost 3 cents to ride the bus. You'd get a quarter and go down there and get filled up. You had to back away from the table. – *Robert McAlpine, Cleveland (East 55th Street)*

I worked in Gray Drugstore at Fourth and Prospect downtown. I worked at the counter for 12-and-a-half cents an hour. They served hamburgers and cheeseburgers, hot dogs, sodas, soda pop, chocolate Coke, cherry Coke, vanilla Coke, and phosphates, which were the big thing back then. – *Marge Skof*

TRAY CHIC: the cafeteria experience drew them in at the Blue Boar. What you saw was what you got.

SOUVENIRS: Mills Restaurant gave away things like baseball schedules and toothpick holders for those who wanted to hang on to the experience.

CAFETERIAS

Places where you pushed along your tray and picked your meal items make for fond memories. Good food and a good value were the reason people patronized downtown places such as Mills Restaurant on Euclid Avenue, the Forum, and the Colonnade. In 1931, the opening of the Forum in Cleveland was featured in *American Restaurant Magazine*, which noted that the place served more than 5,000 people a day.

At Mills Cafeteria, I had one set meal that I always ordered, and I remember my grandmother being upset because it was pricey— $1.59. I always got pot roast with gravy and a sagey bread stuffing, with potatoes, gravy, and coleslaw. They had phenomenal coleslaw, which must have had sugar and whipped cream in it. – *Rita M. Grabowski, Cleveland (West Side)*

If we didn't have lunch at Higbee's, we'd go to Mills Cafeteria, which I loved. They had great old-time waiters who were very polite and would carry your tray to the table. I always got orange drink and macaroni and cheese. – *Carol Lally Metz, Cleveland (East Side)*

FEASTING WITH WINDMILLS: postcards from Mills Restaurant noted that it was "famous for good food and interested service." That's saying something, when a place seats 650.

Pat Bertman Mazoh grew up in the food industry. Her father founded the business that is today called Joe Bertman Foods but was originally the Bertman Pickle Company. At first the company was located in a garage behind the family home at East 147th and Kinsman. "I ate at Mills all the time when I was a kid," Mazoh says. "When I was about eight years old, my routine was going to lunch at Mills Cafeteria, followed by my mother going to the May Company to shop. She parked me at the May Company playground for children, which I hated."

DINERS

Diners around Cleveland may be known as much for who ate there as what was served there. All-day places included the legendary Tony's Diner, where some of Cleveland's politicians met in the mornings. In fact, about 40 million television viewers got a load of Tony's Diner in Cleveland when Tom Snyder of the *Tomorrow Show* interviewed then mayor Dennis Kucinich there. Tony's Diner opened at 3312 West 117th Street in 1947.

At diners around the city, the lunch crowd piled in for a quick bite, and night owls took their places on stools at the counter to grab casual meals and endless cups of coffee.

DINER BELLE: Tony's Diner on West 117th Street became a neighborhood institution after its 1947 opening.

BEFORE BEARDEN'S: in 1940, Jackson's Diner was a Rocky River drive-in; it later became the site of Bearden's.

My grandmother, Flora Kirk, owned Kirk's Diner on Ivanhoe Road in Cleveland during the 1950s. My mom was the manager. She'd drive home after the breakfast rush to drive me to elementary school, and would bring me a doughnut to eat in the car. They were the best. My favorite was a cream-filled one, shaped like an éclair and topped with chocolate frosting. – *Carol Lally Metz*

Growing up, Stills Diner on Detroit Avenue in Lakewood made the biggest impression on me. I always liked to believe it had been a real rail car before (even though I knew better). It became one of my favorite burger places. As a grade-school kid, I used to sit there with my parents, eyes glazed over, waiting for our order to arrive, and I'd imagine speeding down the tracks to some new big city and its waiting rail yard.

Later, I'd meet my junior high rock 'n' roll bandmates there to fuel up early for a Saturday of fun with a burger breakfast. In high school, my girlfriend and I were regulars. After college, although the ownership had changed, I'd sit at one of the eight red counter stools thinking about the original cook, Floyd, and the simpler days of the sixties.

After living in Oklahoma for 20 years and finding nothing even close to "The Diner" anywhere in my travels, I wrote a poem about those wonderful but long-done days, punctuated by chowing down on a couple of well-done cheeseburgers with a side of home fries. – *George Ghetia*

CAR CULTURE: Kenny King's had a casual, relaxed atmosphere and a menu that appealed to all ages.

I went to John Marshall High School in Cleveland, and a hangout was the diner at West 117th. A lot of hot cars hung out there in the 1950s and 1960s. The diner sold hot dogs and root beer floats. And at Chatfield and West 150th, there was a diner with a train that ran around inside the place. – *Jim Kovach, Cleveland*

CHAIN GANG

The sixties was the era when fast-food places flew up faster than we could visit them. They might not have been unique to Cleveland, but they certainly left their impression on the baby boomers.

> I must have been in seventh grade and was staying the weekend at a friend's house. Her father had a 1964 Chrysler Imperial—gold—and we drove out to what was one of the first Arby's in Cleveland. I started eating them and couldn't stop. I ate five of them. – *Rita M. Grabowski*

> Beef Corral in Lakewood was the first place I ever tasted barbecue sauce. We'd never had it on anything else. – *George Ghetia*

> McDonald's was a special treat. I used to think, "This is the best thing in the world— fries in a bag!" – *Michael Sanson, Bay Village*

CASUAL CHICK

Kenny King's is fondly remembered for its carhops, its burgers, its toy chest for kids who cleaned their plates, and, of course, Colonel Sanders Kentucky Fried Chicken.

> After high school football games and dances, we all went to Kenny King's Restaurant and Drive-In. It was near or on Lake Shore Boulevard, near the city of Euclid. We ordered cheeseburgers and Cokes. In my mind, those were the best cheeseburgers ever. I can still taste them. On Monday morning, everybody would gossip about who had been seen with whom at Kenny King's on Friday or Saturday night.
> – *Carol Lally Metz*

> At our Kenny King's, the one on Rocky River, you had to be in the clean plate club to get your toy.
> – *Bob Krummert, Cleveland (West Park)*

> We had Kentucky Fried Chicken, no matter what family event we were having. My mother would always say, "Should I stop and get the Kentucky Fried Chicken?" She just assumed that's what we would have for every food occasion.
> – *Lyn Byrd*

KING OF THE ROAD: Hilliard Road, that is—Kenny King's in Rocky River, 1966.

BAG-O-BURGERS: "Buy 'em by the Sack" was the slogan at White Castle.

NOT A FARM: city-dwelling fans of Red Barn recall its fried chicken, burgers, and fish.

QUICK BITES: FAST-FOOD DEBUTS

In the 1960s, as baby boomers reached their teens, the number of fast-food restaurants in the U.S. almost tripled.

1952: Chicken Delight hatches in Illinois

1954: Burger King is born in Miami

1955: Colonel Sanders Kentucky Fried Chicken opens in Kentucky

McDonald's is born on April 15, in Des Plaines, Illinois

1956: Burger Chef starts in Indianapolis

1958: Pizza Hut opens in Wichita, Kansas

1962: Taco Bell starts up in Downey, California

1969: Wendy's makes its debut in Columbus, Ohio

Long John Silver's Fish 'n' Chips opens in Lexington, Kentucky

☞

MIAMI NICE: Royal Castle started out in Florida in 1938 and made its name here with burgers and birch beer.

HAMBURGER HANGOUTS

At drive-ins, at lunch counters and snack bars, we loved our burgers. We're talking about the culinary artistry of a juicy, pungent, tooth-pleasing burger tucked between pieces of really great bread, garnished with crispy or grilled onions, tangy ketchup, gooey cheese, or any number of other add-ons.

At least one Clevelander played a part in the invention of this casual classic. A Salisbury steak by any other name is a hamburger patty, and we can thank one of our own for that creation. Dr. James H. Salisbury, a Cleveland physician who lived nearly 100 years ago, invented and named the Salisbury steak. It was nothing more or less than a ground-beef patty with minced onions and other seasonings. Dr. Salisbury was buried in Lake View Cemetery in 1906, but the Salisbury steak lives on.

Jeffrey Tennyson, in his book *Hamburger Heaven*, has delved into the beginnings of those burgers we all love so much. While Northeast Ohio isn't exactly a fast-food fertile crescent, Lake Shore Boulevard was nevertheless the local cradle of burger civilization in two instances. Cleveland's first Manners Drive-In sprung up at 17655 Lake Shore Boulevard. By 1964, there were about 30 Manners Big Boy restaurants in the area. The first Cleveland-area McDonald's arrived on the scene around 1961, at 16910 Lake Shore Boulevard.

As for the inventor of the hamburger itself, accounts vary. Many concessionaires vie for the title of hamburger honcho. It may have been Frank Menches from Akron who sold ground-meat patties at a county fair in Akron (1892), or Charlie Nagreen at a county fair in Wisconsin (1885), or Louis Lassen in New Haven, Connecticut (1900), or an unnamed food vendor—perhaps Fletcher Davis of Athens, Texas—at the St. Louis World's Fair (1904).

TWICE THE FUN: double-patty burgers were on the menu at Manners Big Boy.

By 1964, there were about 30 Manners Big Boy restaurants in the area.

But is it really the burgers we remember? In some cases, it seems to be the sauce, the grilled onions, or the service.

> I tipped my first waitress at the Royal Castle on Chester and East 13th. I thought she looked like Hayley Mills. I left her a nickel. I was six. – *Joe Valencic*

> I remember the Royal Castle next to the Broadview Theater on Pearl Road. I ended up there with my grandmother on Saturdays. They had very serviceable home fries, birch beer, and burgers similar to White Castle sliders, but I don't remember them coming with holes punched in them. I'd always take the pickle off the top. I was quite a methodical child, and had this specific system set up. – *Rita M. Grabowski*

> In the late '60s, Paige's, on the corner of 79th and Superior, was the hangout for hamburgers. Maybe they had wings, too, but we only ate hamburgers and french fries. – *Dorothy Bell*

MEMORIES OF MANNERS

Bob Wian invented the double-decker hamburger (two burgers with a center bun soaking up the juices) out in California in 1937. Wian's first Big Boy Hamburgers outlet was in Glendale. In 1946, he began making franchise agreements around the country, and franchise operators added their own names to the restaurants. Hence, Manners Big Boy in Cleveland.

Marge Skof, who opened the Manners on Route 20 in Painesville in 1955 as assistant manager, recalls the menu: "The Big Boy was the big thing, and Manners had that secret Big Boy Sauce which nobody could seem to copy. There were also hamburgers and cheeseburgers, fries, milk shakes, and soft freeze. That's when those machines first came out—Taylor machines. I think they were first brought into service with Manners and Kenny King's. They were hell to clean out, too."

She gives strawberry pie fans a peek into the making of that famous Manners dessert. "Manners got known for its strawberry pie. We used to make them. It was the special glaze made by Pratt and Webb Pie Company in the 1950s—a strawberry glaze. We got the strawberries fresh from California; the ones from California were the best. We cleaned them, and we made the crust. And don't forget the whipped cream on top. We went through plenty of whipped cream."

☞
MEAT AT MANNERS: with its drive-in design and popular burgers, Manners was as much a meeting place as it was an eating place.

PRICE CHECK

1921: A hamburger at White Castle cost 5 cents.

1954: A hamburger at Burger King cost 18 cents.

1958: A hamburger at Burger Chef cost 15 cents.

1968: A Big Mac at McDonald's cost 49 cents.

HIP SIP: gulping a Big Ghoulardi drink was the thing to do at Manners.

HEY GROUP COOL IT! DRINK A MANNERS BiG GHOULARDi ©

Ghoulardi's own secret formula. And made only by Manners. Weirdly wonderful. 16 ounces of delicious devilment. Makes you feel glad you're alive. 35¢

ERIC SILK SCREEN 439-1944

© COPYRIGHT STORER BROADCASTING CO.

Manners Big Boy on Mayfield was the hangout when I was in high school. My father was good friends with Mr. Manners. You couldn't buy the sauce they used, and he gave me three jars of it. That's what I wanted for my birthday. – *Sheila Bellamy*

I loved Big Boys. In high school, we would go to Manners at Warrensville, Northfield, and Van Aken Boulevard. I loved the Big Boy Sauce. – *Lilli Lief*

Manners had wonderful sauce for its hamburgers. After a while, you could buy a jar of it. – *Therese Hummer*

Manners at night was a drive-in deal. We never got out of the car. – *Sam DeGaetano, Cleveland*

Manners at Warrensville and Chagrin was a hangout. They had carhops, and were famous for strawberry pie. – *Karen Perry, Shaker Heights*

At Manners in Lakewood, I loved the Diamond Jim—ham and mozzarella cheese on a long-jong bun with lettuce and tomato. And I loved the strawberry pie.
– *Laura Budny, Lakewood*

MEMORIES OF MAWBY'S

While we liked the burgers, we loved the onions.

When I was 12, and up through high school, we used to go to Mawby's for the best hamburgers that I ever had. It was at Cedar Center, a long narrow diner, almost. You'd sit at the counter. They made hamburgers at a long grill. And they had the best grilled onions. It was just a plain, greasy grill that they threw the onions on, and a whole row of people were standing there cooking the hamburgers. The bun would be hot, and the hamburgers were thin. – *Lilli Lief*

Mawby's was a great hangout, and it lasted longer than high school. They had the greatest grilled onions and late-night burgers. I tried to do the onions at home and couldn't do it. Rather than crunchy, they were soft. I'm sure they were steamed before putting them on the grill. I know they put paprika on them.
– *Sam DeGaetano*

Mawby's was my favorite burger—not for the burger, for the onions. Their grilled onions were absolutely heaven. I have no idea how they made them, but I know they put paprika on them. – *Pat Bertman Mazoh*

UNDER THE COUNTER

As we sat at lunch counters, soda fountains, diners, and burger joints, we needed a place to stash our used chewing gum.

Steve Presser, who likes to collect unusual items, says, "I wish I would have gotten the counter at Mawby's. Not for the countertop, but for the bubblegum underneath. There were hundreds and thousands of pieces of it." Favorites of the age were probably Teaberry, Beeman's, Clove, Chiclets, Dentyne, Wild Cherry, and Black Jack gum. Maybe even some of that exotic Fan Tan gum.

Mawby's had wonderful burgers. I heard about them when I was spending summers working at the dry cleaners at Warrensville/Chagrin/Van Aken when I was in college. Mawby's had giant hamburgers, roughly made. When you picked them up they were fragrant and juicy, juicy as if you'd made them at home. – *Pat Fernberg*

Mawby's used to have the best burgers. The grilled onions and the hamburgers were out of this world. – *Anna Chenin*

MEMORIES OF BEARDEN'S

You may remember going to Bearden's in Lakewood or on Rocky River Drive, having one of their burgers with peanut butter on it. The Bearden's in Rocky River still survives today.

At Bearden's on Rocky River Drive, I remember the onion rings. It was the pre–french fry era. How french fries ever won out over really good onion rings, I don't understand. – *Bob Krummert*

I graduated from Bay Village High School, class of 1953. At our 50th class reunion, one of the things we had to do was go to lunch at Bearden's in Rocky River. In the fifties in Bay Village, there was no place to go to eat after football games, so everybody would go to Bearden's. At the time, they still had carhops. You pulled the car in, found a spot, placed your order, and they brought it out to you. Before it was Bearden's, it was called Jackson's. – *Marie DeLuca Sandru, Bay Village*

WHAT THE RESTAURANT WRITERS SAID

Heck's (Beachcliff Market Square, 19300 Detroit Avenue, Rocky River): One may be surprised to learn that in 1974, Heck's specialized only in hamburgers. Today, its famed burgers take second billing to the culinary creations that part owner John Saile likes to call "American nouvelle."

– *Dining In–Cleveland,* 1982

"Their grilled onions were absolutely heaven."

Department Store Dining

Jim McConnell, whose career in department store food service started in Dallas, recalls his first glimpse of Higbee's Silver Grille, where he worked as food service director beginning in 1983:

> I fell in love with it at first sight. I came up here just for a courtesy interview. They asked me up from Dallas and I had no intention of moving. They flew me up and I walked in the day before to look around. I saw that Grille, and fell in love. The feeling has lasted until this day. It was a great love affair.

McConnell stayed there until it closed. "Before I left, I locked all the china plates and other memorabilia in a storeroom. I felt that some day, because it was an historic landmark, it would be needed." He gives a rough estimate that about 8 percent of the clientele worked at Higbee's, 65 to 68 percent were people who ate there regularly, and the rest were shoppers or those who came there for a special meal. Among the latter were many of Cleveland's young people.

HIGBEE *Silver Grille*

STERLING REPUTATION: women who came downtown to shop could catch a fashion show and snag a Maurice Salad at Higbee's Silver Grille.

FIFTH FLOOR, FOOD DEPARTMENT: hungry shoppers made memories as well as purchases when they stopped at the May Company's restaurants, including the Spanish Room.

Mostly, I remember going to the Silver Grille for a certain occasion, a birthday or a friend's birthday. My mother would make me get all dressed up with gloves, pearls, patent leather shoes, and my best clothes. I remember the little cardboard stoves, and chicken pot pie. The waitresses wore uniforms, and were all so friendly. They catered a lot to children. I remember how lovely the room was decorated. It was like a palace to me, because we lived in an apartment building. – *Helen Weinberger, Cleveland (Near East Side)*

Given my druthers, I would go downtown and eat at the Silver Grille every day, even when I was older and had my first job in display at the May Company. Those muffins—I would kill for them. And the Welsh rarebit with almonds. – *Rita M. Grabowski*

When we shopped downtown, we ate at the Silver Grille, and the Pronto Room, the fast-serve place at Higbee's with a fixed menu. – *Stephen G. Michaelides*

Other department stores had memory-making restaurants as well. Here are a few recollections.

MAY COMPANY

Because I went to public school, I had different days off than my sisters did at Catholic school. My mother and I would sneak downtown and go out to lunch at the May Company cafeteria. It was on the first floor, toward the back. You walked up a little ramp. We had hamburgers and butterscotch sundaes, always. The butterscotch sundaes were served in little aluminum dishes, and the butterscotch could make your throat hurt, it was that wild. It was our little secret. We'd try on hats and look at lingerie. Lunch with your mom welds a friendship that has nothing to do with what you ate. – *Pat Fernberg*

HALLE BROTHERS

The Geranium Room at Halle's was well known for their salads. I usually got the cheese omelet. – *Anna Chenin*

TAYLOR'S

I went to Taylor's—this must have been in the fifties—and I don't know if they specifically served tea, but I remember having finger sandwiches. That was an out-of-body experience for somebody of my ethnicity. – *Rita M. Grabowski*

"That was an out-of-body experience for somebody of my ethnicity."

OUTSIDE STEAKS: Ted Miclau's Black Angus offered "charcoal steaks" at Playhouse Square. In 1964, you could dine al fresco.

MENU TALK

In days past, steak size was apparently a gender thing on menus. Old Austria, 20412 Center Ridge Road in Rocky River, offered "man-sized" chopped sirloin steak with onion rings ($1.85).

Meanwhile, at Al Maharas Steak House, the "Ladies Delight" filet mignon sold for $3.25, while the Maharas Favorite "For a Great Big He Man" went for $4.25.

Steaks of the Past: Big on Beef

Meat and potatoes were serious business for Cleveland restaurant goers, and nowhere were they more serious than in the city's steak houses. Here are some thick and juicy memories.

My first grown-up restaurant experience was going to Jim's Steak House on my sixth birthday. I had never seen a salad like the one I was served—a slice of iceberg lettuce with two cherry tomatoes and orangey French dressing. I think I drowned my ground round with a "Roy Rogers." – *Joe Valencic*

I must have been nine or ten when we went to the Black Angus for dinner. I remember the dress I wore, a pink dress with a petticoat that could shred cabbage. I remember the Black Angus being the damned coolest experience on the planet. I ordered filet. And it was well done. I remember asking for ketchup and steak sauce. The waitstaff was just thrilling. I was nine going on 30. I'm sure I ordered a Shirley Temple. – *Rita M. Grabowski*

Everyplace I went, I had the same thing: steak or roast beef; a baked potato or mashed potatoes; peas and carrots or creamed spinach; whatever salad they had, with French dressing; and Coca-Cola. I ordered steak at the Terrace Room in the Statler, at the Alpine Village, and at the Theatrical. – *Sheila Bellamy*

HAT'S RIGHT: steaks and spirits were the order of the day at the Brown Derby.

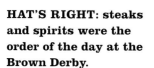

Larisa Lucaci was born in Romania and came to Cleveland in the 1950s. "When we first came to Cleveland, we were not oriented to restaurants at all. We had small children. I think the Black Angus downtown was our first Cleveland restaurant experience."

The famous Maharas Steak House on Wade park featured Al's "That Salad." Al cut his own steaks in the basement and stored the prime quarters of beef in a walk-in cooler down there. During all the years of his operation, Al employed the same bartender, Ernie Coates, and on weekends the same piano player, Bill. His waitresses were among the best—they loved working there because the elite trade were handsome tippers. – *Aaron Jacobson*

My most memorable meal in Cleveland was the surf-and-turf at Brown Derby. I had never heard of it before, and thought it was a wonderful invention to serve meat and fish on the same plate. – *Laurie Orr, Lakewood*

Our family did not eat out as a family. When I was in high school, for special occasions a group of girls would go to Brown Derby and that was a real treat. – *Eileen Murray, North Olmsted*

**STEAKOUT:
Jim's Steak House with
its waterfront view was
a Cleveland dining
tradition.**

Have Fork, Will Travel

Dining in restaurants allows us to get a taste of the world. Food is a way we identify ourselves, and we express our culture through our cooking. As Cuyahoga Community College professor of anthropology and urban studies Mark Lewine notes, "We're the talking primate, but we're also the cooking primate." Lewine also happens to be director of the Center for Community Research. He adds, "Different ethnic groups focus on food differently. I grew up in a Jewish household with Mediterranean flavor. Most restaurant owners will tell you that quite a few of them depend on maintaining good relationships with Jewish customers."

"We're the talking primate, but we're also the cooking primate."

The Cleveland Press

olde time recipes

By BARBARA BRATEL
Foods Editor

RETRO RECIPES: cookbooks allowed Clevelanders to indulge in armchair travel to a different time or place.

IF YOU WOOD: carvings, decor, and cuisine all pointed to Polynesia to provide an ethnic dining experience at the Kon-Tiki.

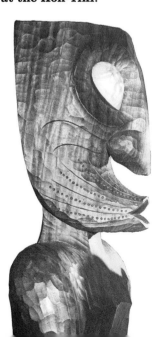

In the past, eating ethnic cuisine in a restaurant probably meant eating a different rendition of what Mom cooked at home. If you were Italian, you tended to frequent Italian restaurants. If you were Hungarian, you went to Hungarian restaurants. Jim Kovach, who grew up on the West Side of Cleveland, remembers going to Bit of Budapest, 6355 Pearl Road. "We were Hungarian, and my dad liked it because it was Old Country."

Cleveland's tastes reflect a culinary melting pot. In their 1970 *Nationality Cookbook Swap & Shop* (a souvenir of the first All Nationality Fair at St. Joseph High), authors Bill Randle and Tony Petkovsek provided a cross-section of Cleveland's ethnic cuisines. Listeners to "Tony's Polka Party" on WXEN tuned in for featured recipes of the week, such as pierogi, matzo ball soup, and strudel dough. On WERE, a popular feature among Bill Randle's "Ask Your Neighbor" radio audience was the sharing of recipes such as potato dumplings, Hungarian pastry, beet soup, and Irish soda bread.

If you grew up thinking pierogies were just naked ravioli with a Polish accent, you've no doubt had a chance to rethink that. When Parma Pierogies opened at 7707 West Ridgewood Drive, with its pink flamingo logo, it was offering Cleveland culture on a plate. Janet Beighle French, who served as food editor of the *Plain Dealer* for 25 years starting in 1963, says, "When I came here, I had never tasted pierogies, never seen kielbasa or pastitsio."

Recipes also allow us to travel back in time. During the nation's bicentennial year, Barbara Bratel, foods editor at the *Cleveland Press*, featured "Olde Time Recipes" in the paper's food section. These were compiled in *The Cleveland Press Olde Time Recipes*, and included farmhouse pot roast, chicken à la king, and a Shaker recipe for Ohio lemon pie.

FIRST TASTE OF THE WORLD

Today, according to research done by the National Restaurant Association, restaurants are where most people get their first taste of an ethnic cuisine outside their own culture. The most popular cuisines are Mexican, Chinese, and Italian. What we call ethnic cooking today used to be referred to as international cuisine, and many of us got our first taste of it in a restaurant. Here's a brief snapshot of Cleveland's offerings, as several people describe their memorable restaurant experiences.

MISSING LINKS: The Austrian-German "wurstmarket" buffet at Old Austria in April 1969 was a sausage festival with food, music, and dancing.

Casey Claytor came to Cleveland in 1954, and recalls his first food experience in the Glenville area: "My earliest food memory is a restaurant at 102nd and St. Clair, Dearing's Barbecue. He opened up a barbecue pit, a barbecue stand, there. He used to trim the ribs after he cooked them, trimmed them to take off all the fat that he could. That left quite a good bit of lean. He would give the fat away."

In California in the 1940s, Trader Vic's blazed the trail for restaurants offering Polynesian-inspired food and rum-rich drinks such as Planter's Punch and the Zombie. Clevelanders took to the theme in a big way when the Kon-Tiki opened in the Sheraton-Cleveland Hotel. "I remember going to the Kon-Tiki for several showers," says Clevelander Jan DeLucia. "I had fruit salad with sherbet and coconut."

KIEFER'S KEEPERS: customers kept returning to Kiefer's Tavern for the schmoozing as much as the schnitzel.

GERMAN RESTAURANTS

Oddly enough, our St. Patrick's Day ritual always included a stop at Kiefer's, a German Restaurant owned by the very Irish Frank Gaul and his wife. Located at 25th and Detroit, it was convenient to the parade route, and all the politicos went there to grab a quick sandwich, shake some hands, and do a bit of campaigning for the May primaries. I was probably in that German restaurant once a year, but never tasted so much as a schnitzel because I was too busy eating corned beef sandwiches on rye after the parade. But being in that giant restaurant was an event all unto itself.
– *Miriam Carey*

My earliest ethnic restaurant experience was the Hofbrau Haus. I enjoyed the noodles, and soup. – *Anna Chenin*

Old Austria was a customer of ours for many years. They used to buy 100-pound bags of potatoes. Carrying those up the steps was a challenge. – *Carl LoPresti*

I liked the kielbasa and sauerkraut at Old Austria. – *Laura Budny*

SPELLING LESSONS

Be thankful that Cleveland's ethnic food specialties didn't show up on those spelling tests you took in school.

The Polish favorite of half-moon–shaped, filled noodle dumplings is spelled *pierogie*, but you might have seen it spelled as *pierogy*, too. If you're talking about the small Russian turnovers filled with cheese, meat, fruit, or vegetables, though, you'll want to spell them *pirozhki*—unless you're talking about the bigger, entrée-sized version, in which case it's *pirogi*.

Maybe you're a big fan of kielbasa, Polish sausage. If so, you'll eat it even if it's spelled *kielbasy*, or, depending on your own ethnic background, *kolbasz* or *kolbasa*. Just don't get yourself into a situation where you've got to spell it for academic credit.

Ditto for that strudel-like, tissue-thin pastry dough that's made into yummy Greek and Middle Eastern specialties such as baklava and spanakopita. Whether you spell it *phyllo* or *filo*, it still tastes great.

☞

HIGH-BRAU: Hofbrau Haus offered the German dining experience in a themed setting that made for good times and good food.

EXCELLENT MEMORIES: The waiters at New York Spaghetti House could always get your order right without jotting it down.

CHINESE RESTAURANTS

My family's favorite celebration place was a Chinese restaurant on St. Clair, under the bridge. We used to come all the way to Cleveland, even before I-71 was built. There were five of us, so it was probably expensive, too. We always used to get the dinner for six, to make sure we had leftovers to take home. – *Lyn Byrd*

I remember Chinese Garden restaurant near West 117th and Clifton. As good as the egg rolls, wonton soup, and spare ribs were, I usually filled up on French bread and real butter before the main event. – *George Ghetia*

My first Chinese food was at a restaurant near the corner of 79th and Cedar—the State Restaurant. I had ham fried rice. – *Dorothy Bell*

ITALIAN RESTAURANTS

Whether it was a teen hangout where one could get a first taste of pizza, or a celebration spot for Italian specialties, Clevelanders have a fondness for Italian food.

The best pizza I ever had was at Tony's at Kamm's. I grew up in St. Mel's Parish. To get money to get pizza at Tony's, we'd go Christmas caroling door-to-door, saying we were from the St. Mel's Athletic Fund. It was an early entrepreneurial bait-and-switch adventure. We were from St. Mel's, we were athletes, and we did have a fund—to get money to feed ourselves at Tony's. A lot of people would give us a dollar. In 1957, that was a lot for four kids singing. We were pretty good singers. We were all in the choir—and we were all fast. We did one song, and got out. – *Bob Krummert*

I had my 16th birthday party at Roman Gardens in Little Italy. My friends sneaked in a birthday cake. – *Karen Perry*

Our family's favorite celebration restaurant was Roman Gardens in Little Italy—glamorous, sophisticated, and, oh-SO-Italian. I pretended I was Italian. – *Sali A. McSherry*

Hot Food Comin' Through
Working in Restaurants

The restaurant life isn't all glamour. It's hard work, long hours, and the chow isn't always what you might expect.

> It's interesting what chefs eat—McDonald's or the Big Egg. We used to go there after working at Top of the Town. You got out late, and then went there for a big breakfast. – *Jan DeLucia*

A peek behind the scenes at some of Cleveland's restaurants, now closed, makes us realize the level of commitment the restaurant business requires.

SALADS, ROLLS, AND FINGER BOWLS

"I still like the restaurant business," says Doris Urbansky who, with her husband Tom, operated Miller's Dining Room in Lakewood. Her parents started the restaurant in 1950, and the family ran it until 1989, when they sold it. A fire destroyed the restaurant in 1995.

> I'd go back if I could take it. It wasn't because we didn't like it that we quit, but Tom was 67 and I was 65. Working that many hours, from 45 to 65 hours a week, is a long time. I was 27 when I started. That's a long stretch. We didn't do a thing. Everything was work. I had our daughter three days before Easter Sunday, and by Easter Sunday I was back at the restaurant. We had hired somebody to run the kitchen and it didn't work out too well.

For 39 years, she says, she and her husband never went anyplace. "When my daughter graduated from college, that's the first day we took off."

What it takes to succeed, Urbansky says, is the ability to run the entire restaurant.

> I think you have to run the whole thing, like Herman Pirchner did. We used to go to his place [Alpine Village] for birthdays before we were in business. I was quite

OF WORLD CUISINE AND WHIRLED CUISINE

In his introduction to *The Hilton International Cookbook* (1960), which features recipes from the chefs of the Hilton Hotels, hotelier Conrad N. Hilton writes, "Across a dinner table, people from different countries discover each other's ideas, opinions, and cultural backgrounds. Through this interchange we learn to understand each other better, and in a small way we promote world peace."

Among the recipes customers requested are several from Cleveland's Statler Hilton—Breast of Turkey with Sauce Paulette, Corn Fritters, Crissfield Crabmeat a la Dewey, Beef Stew with Red Wine, Old Fashioned Chicken Pot Pie, and Creamy Oyster Stew. Also, there's a dessert recipe for Thin Pancakes, with the recipe note, "At the Hotel Statler in Cleveland, these pancakes are made in an electric blender."

MUSIC AND MENU: Herman Pirchner (back row, second from right) presented entertainment as well as edibles at his Alpine Village Restaurant in the 1930s.

young, a teenager, when they started having the shows. They used to have a platform stage that raised up and the gals would dance. I'll never forget, because Herman Pirchner used to carry about a couple dozen steins of beer, and come right down the middle of the stage. He'd put one foot out and do a dance carrying this beer. We were sorry to see that place go.

RHAPSODY IN BREW

Doris Urbansky's estimate of the number of beer steins Herman Pirchner hefted was not far off. According to Pirchner, he used to stack up 25 of them. It was all part of the show. "When Prohibition was repealed, I wanted to cash in. I'd carry steins of beer in a pyramid and slide across the dance floor in a baseball slide, and jump up without spilling a drop—hardly."

The rising dance floor was an idea Pirchner got from seeing a mechanical car lift. The 360-seat Alpine Village brought in well-known vaudeville acts as well as streamlined versions of Broadway shows and operettas. Its Continental menu featured steaks and chops. "My family has been in the restaurant business ever since the 14th century," he says. "I was one of 15 children, and 8 of them ended up in the restaurant business. It's a business that demands a lot of time and love. The love you get back is when you see people having fun, enjoying themselves." Pirchner

STEIN WAY: restaurateur Herman Pirchner was renowned for stacking up more than two dozen filled beer steins in a pyramid and sliding across the dance floor with them.

BOY ABOUT TOWN: these Big Boy statues congregated at the Manners Big Boy Training Center, 16201 Euclid Avenue, in 1973.

HOPPING TO IT: in 1955, carhops brought the food right to your window at the Manners Drive-In, 385 Turney Road.

also operated the Eldorado Club, which was jumping from 11 p.m. until 6 a.m. "At five or six in the morning, the club was still filled with people," he says.

BELIEVING IN MIRACLES

Gary Grabowski speaks about opening Miracles in Tremont. "It was actually a piece of property my uncle had, a rental that he originally rented out to Dennis Kucinich for his campaign headquarters. I grew up in the area, and we thought it was ripe for a renaissance. We were among the first landowners who renovated their properties." The restaurant was known for its potato pancakes. "I had a food scientist work with me on the recipe," Grabowski says. "He refined it. Our food scientist was from Minor's. He used to come to the restaurant and have lunch, and loved our potato pancakes."

MINDING YOUR MANNERS

Marge Skof, who served as president of the Northeast Ohio Restaurant Association for two years in the late 1960s, was assistant manager of Manners Big Boy when it opened in Painesville in May 1955. "We had carhops, and a staff of around 30. Their ages ranged from 18 to 25. The carhop was a new innovation in the restaurant business. They all learned on the job. They wore black slacks and white shirts." Later, though, the burger training got more formal. "They started a Manners Big Boy Training School on U.S. Route 20, Euclid Avenue. They took the waitresses there and trained them, and had manager training. There was also a test kitchen there where they came up with new menu ideas."

"I had a food scientist work with me on the recipe."

STOREHOUSE OF MEMORIES: adults favored the Welsh rarebit, liver and onions, or other specialties, but kids lucky enough to be taken to eat at Higbee's Silver Grille remember the doll-sized portions of lunch presented in small buffets, little stoves, or trucks.

SILVER THRILL

If there's one restaurant that made an impression on the children of Cleveland, it's Higbee's Silver Grille, which offered kids' lunches served over the years in small buffets, little stoves, and trucks. Jim McConnell was the restaurant's last food service director, from 1983 until its closing on December 31, 1990. "The day we closed, we did not drop a beat. People on the team were absolutely fantastic. They knew in November that we were going to close. I don't think a single person left. Many had been there for 15 or 20 years."

As for those little lunches for kids, he says, "We always prided ourselves on the kids' menu. We also tried to be on the cutting edge. Sometimes we failed miserably. Around 1986, we got into this big heart-healthy kick and geared our menu around that. We had heart-healthy items, no-sugar-added muffins, fat-free foods, and so on. It ended up being about 2 percent of our business. I thought it was a great idea and we ran with it, but people wanted liver and onions and meat loaf, Welsh rarebit and the Maurice Salad. And, of course, the kids' lunches served over the years in buffets, stoves, and trucks."

ICE-CREAM DREAMS: the colorful interior and fantasy-inspired sundae names were part of the coolness at Boukair's.

COOL CUSTOMERS

When Salwa Boukair of Boukair's SeeSweets began working in her late husband's ice-cream business in 1965, it had already been in existence since 1932. "It started on Hough Avenue," she says, "and then moved downtown to Euclid Avenue." That was in the 1950s. The restaurant's decor sticks in the mind as much as the menu does, Salwa recalls,

Everybody thought it was like Las Vegas, because of so many different colors and lights and dishes my husband designed that were made by a company in Pennsylvania. He also named the sundaes—Lover's Delight, Temple of Love, and Cof-Fiesta. Whipped cream for the sundaes was made on the spot. We were whipping it every five minutes.

Her husband, Moe Boukair, and his brother George were partners. "They both did the ice cream. It was like an assembly line, one doing the bananas, one doing the cherries." The downtown restaurant closed in 1972. "I'm proud we left a nice name. My husband was a good man."

A FROZEN ASSET

Stouffer's was a Cleveland tradition long before its line of frozen foods was in every grocer's frozen food case. Jan DeLucia, program manager for the Hospitality Management Department at Cuyahoga Community College, had years of experience in food service before becoming involved in education. She says of her experience at Stouffer's as a food production manager, "It was a fascinating place to work. It set a lot of careers in motion. Their systems were so good that when I went to other jobs, it was like I was a genius. I cannot tell you how many times I have been pulled to the front of the line because I had Stouffer's experience."

COOL TASTE OF CLEVELAND: frozen favorites roll off the Stouffer's Frozen Foods assembly line.

BUT WILL IT FLY?
Workers at Schreiber Catering at the airport prepared meals for airline passengers, who got a taste of Marie Schreiber's food in 1958.

WILL IT FLY?

Another Stouffer's alum is Doris Urbansky of Miller's. "I graduated from Western Reserve, and was a dietician at Stouffer's. I went to Pittsburgh and New York City for Stouffer's, and worked at the Fifth Avenue restaurant." After that, she took over the airline catering operations for Marie Schreiber. "Marie used to do the airlines' food. We had a whole tray, and everything fit within it in little dishes. We used to do terrific meals—Swiss steak, beef tenderloin, we even baked our own rolls. We were on Brookpark Road, which at the time was across the street from the airport, in an old farmhouse."

Many of the Miller's traditions were inherited from the previous owner, Mrs. Kaase. Among them were the finger bowls, and the trays of signature rolls and salads. For many years, Miller's Dining Room did not serve alcohol, also a part of the restaurant's legacy. "Mrs. Kaase never served alcohol. We had it about 15 years, but we never pushed it. When we got the license, nobody knew we were applying for it."

Chicken à la king in a potato basket, leg of lamb, and beef short ribs were among the restaurant's most popular entrees, but nothing rivals the reputation of the Miller's sticky buns. "In the roll recipe, we used to use a sugar that you can't buy anymore. This sugar today crusts on the bottom. We used to grease the pans, put the brown sugar on the bottom, and put the melted butter on top of it, and then put the roll in there. Today, the sugar doesn't get caramel-y. It gets sugary instead. Now when I'm making the rolls, I make a syrup instead. I use corn syrup and sugar together." So there you have it.

"In the roll recipe, we used to use a sugar that you can't buy anymore."

WE GIVE EAGLE STAMPS

PAVNY'S
FOOD SHOPPE
12526 Buckeye Road

FRUIT AND VEGETABLES

CREAMER AND DELICATESS

1934 or 34

SPECIALS FOR THURSDAY, FRIDAY & SATURDAY, MARCH 29 - 30 - 3

Fresh Ground Poppy Seed	Sour Cream	Pressed Cottage Cheese	Lekvar	New Walnu
19¢ lb	13¢ pt	6¢ lb	13¢ lb	18¢ Large size 25¢

1932

Food Shopping

**Shopping represents an important step
in the route that our food travels
from farm to table. Perhaps that's why
we've always taken it so seriously.**

A NEIGHBORHOOD TRADITION: Jack Pavny of Pavny's grocery store, which opened in 1932 and operated until the 1960s. "My father never updated the store or had a phone in it," said Rita Pavny Lockman.

We are as connected to our favorite sources for ingredients as we are to our fond food memories. Home delivery isn't as vital today as it was before the car culture kicked in, but it seems some of us miss that right-to-the-door service. Although the world of shopping has evolved, in many cases we can still frequent the stores and markets our mothers patronized. In addition to providing food, these places continue to offer a lasting connection to neighborhoods and childhood. We enter our favorite shops with appetites, and we exit with the anticipation of a great meal to come. Some things never change.

Bringing It All Back Home: Retail Details

Dairies, delis, and small grocery stores were integral parts of our neighborhoods before supermarkets became the shopping places of choice. Once the new ideas caught on, though, things changed quickly. A & P introduced its first supermarket in 1936. Many of us have memories of its house brand, Ann Page, in our pantries at home. We might also remember Heritage House products from Fisher's, or have memories of accompanying our mothers to Bi-Rite, Kroger's, Pick-n-Pay, Fazio's, Rini's, Rego's, Murman's, or a host of small neighborhood stores. Super-

markets went from accounting for 35 percent of food sales in the U.S. in 1950 to 70 percent by 1960.

However, mom-and-pop–style stores remained prevalent in Cleveland's neighborhoods. One example is Pavny's at 12526 Buckeye Road, which was operated by the late Jack and Blanche Pavny from the 1920s until 1969. The family business was started as Greenfeld's Creamery by Louis Greenfeld, who came to the U.S. from Austria-Hungary in 1911. His daughter Blanche grew up in the business, and when she married Jack Pavny in 1926, they took over the creamery. Its name was changed to the Buckeye Heights Creamery & Delicatessen, and then to Pavny's. In 1934, the store was selling rye or Vienna bread for 6 cents a loaf, and pumpkins were a penny a pound.

The idea of chain grocery stores was introduced to Cleveland by the Chandler & Rudd Company, which opened in the 1800s and offered imported specialty foods as well as groceries. The original store on Public Square later moved to another Euclid Avenue location, and then added an outlet at East 55th and Euclid. The company opened more branches in the 1930s, and was one of the first grocery stores in the country to start a system where customers could order groceries by telephone to be delivered. In the 1940s, Chandler & Rudd had four grocery stores.

> My mother shopped at the A & P around the corner, and at Hudak's Meat Market, also around the corner within a short walk of home. She worked at the A & P as a cashier before I was born. I remember she said she had to go to bagging school, to learn how to bag properly so it was compact and balanced and the food was safe. And she had to learn the prices of every item, every week. It was in the early 1940s.
> – Pat Fernberg, Cleveland (Buckeye Road)

> The place I miss the most is Sparkle Market. It was the only food market in Brunswick. That was my first job in high school. I still have a scar from a cut that I got opening Jell-O boxes with a box cutter. – Lyn Byrd, Brunswick

BRAND NEWS: the signage at Otto's Delicatessen, 201 Westlake Road, promoted Old Timer's Ale, Leisy, Bowman Ice Cream, and other brands.

PRICE CHECK:

1934: A dozen eggs cost 17 cents at Pavny's on Buckeye Road.

1950: A dozen eggs cost 39 cents at Heinen's, South Taylor Road.

1968: A 16-ounce Chef Boyardee cheese pizza cost 39 cents at Murman's Super Valu, 19525 Hilliard Road, Rocky River.

FAMILY FOODS: by the time the 1935 edition of the Cleveland City Directory came out, John F. Schulte and Sons at 3404 Lorain Avenue was one of more than 1,750 retail groceries listed in the city.

Heinen's grocery store chain was established in 1929 by Joseph Heinen, who opened a butcher shop in Shaker Heights and later expanded the line of foods he carried. The shop built a reputation for service and cleanliness. Heinen's also opened its first self-serve supermarket on Shaker Square in 1949, with more stores to follow on both the east and west sides of Cleveland.

> Mother shopped at Heinen's on Taylor Road near Cedar. We traveled there by bus. I watched the doughnuts going around in the fat, while she shopped. If I couldn't find her, I'd look in the meat department. It seemed she was always staring into the meat.
> – Linda Goodman Robiner, University Heights

> My mother shopped at Heinen's at Lander. She lived around the block from where the original Heinen's was. Joe Heinen first started with a butcher shop at Chagrin and Lee. My mother thought he was a pretty good butcher.
> – Karen Perry, Shaker Heights

Many Clevelanders went where they got the best deals, which means they shopped around.

> My mother shopped at several stores . . . she read the ads on Wednesday morning and went from store to store, and then came home and started cooking. – Jodi Kanter, Lyndhurst

Convenience counted, too, and when Mom needed an extra gallon of milk or some lunchmeat for tomorrow's lunches, somebody in the family was dispatched to a neighborhood store. Perhaps you remember riding your bike to Lawson's to get orange juice for breakfast. Maybe you recall singing the jingle to yourself as you pedaled like the wind: "Roll on, Big O. Get that juice up to Lawson's in 40 hours. . . ." Michael Sanson, who grew up in Bay Village, recalls that chip-chopped ham from Lawson's was a standard lunch for him. "I probably ate 1,000 of those sandwiches over the years," he says.

Many Clevelanders have ties to the West Side Market, with family members who either shopped there or worked there for generations.

Milenko Budimir recalls doing the family shopping with his father on Saturday mornings at the West Side Market:

WANTING IT ALL: by 1968, we expected our grocery stores to provide variety, convenience, low prices, trading stamps, and, oh, yeah—good food.

ROLL ON, BIG O: we shopped at Lawson's for ice milk, chip dip, and deli meats, but most of us recall the orange juice that rode up here from Florida in 40 hours.

SHOPPING "À LA CART"

Supermarket technology zipped forward from the time the first shopping carts were introduced in 1937 until the first checkout scanners were introduced in 1974. There's even a Cleveland connection to shopping carts. Sort of.

The original one made its debut near Cleveland—Cleveland County, that is, near Oklahoma City. The cart was invented by Silvan N. Goldman, who owned Standard Food Markets and Humpty Dumpty Supermarkets in Oklahoma. He created a wire basket on wheels so shoppers could buy more. The only trouble was, his customers didn't take readily to the idea. Goldman had another good idea, though: He hired male and female models to push the carts around his stores to show shoppers how convenient the carts were.

Today, there are more than 30 million shopping carts in the U.S. Carts have caught on in such a big way that in Illinois, the month of February is designated as "Return Shopping Carts to the Supermarket" month.

The main headquarters for our food supplies was the West Side Market. I particularly recall the tiny poultry store off the aisle from the main produce stands. The store had two sections, both with cold concrete floors; the one had a glass display case filled with eggs, chicken breasts, whole chickens, livers, and other assorted organs. The other section contained cages with an assortment of poultry including chickens, turkeys, ducks, and geese. I remember walking into the caged section behind my father as he negotiated the best chicken he could find. "Too skinny," he'd say, or "This one old, no meat."

He'd finally find one he liked. The guy helping us out would put a wire tag around our chicken's leg and write our names on it. We'd continue shopping and come back in half an hour to pick up our chicken and take him home.

Chicken-buying seems to have made quite an impression on the children of Cleveland, particularly city kids who were not as connected to the land or food sources as their country cousins were. It didn't matter whether they grew up in the 1940s, the 1950s, or later.

I had an aunt who lived in Parma and raised chickens. One of us would go out to State and Snow Road by a couple of streetcars to get chickens and some eggs from Aunt Emma. Her chickens were so delicious.
– *Claire A. Wirt, Cleveland (Northeast)*

When we lived in the old neighborhood, E. 105th and St. Clair, I remember my mother going to a chicken store and picking out a chicken. The chickens were alive and there was sawdust on the floor. They'd cut its head off, and I would get so sick I'd run out of the store. – *Helen Weinberger, Cleveland (Near East Side)*

Deals on Wheels: Foods Delivered to the Door

Not only did the home delivery system bring food right to our doors, it also provided a communications network that connected families to their neighborhoods. The milkman didn't just deliver food: He provided conversation, dispensed advice, and became almost a part of the family.

But milk wasn't the only product brought to our doorstep. Produce, baked goods, ice cream, potato chips, and even groceries were brought to the door.

GROCERIES ON THE GO

Some Clevelanders, moms without cars for instance, had groceries delivered to their houses. Chandler & Rudd, Murman's, and other places were happy to oblige.

> My mother shopped at Borsee's on Memphis Road, then at Mancini's at 117th and Bellaire. They delivered our groceries. When we moved to Rocky River, they still delivered them, because we had 11 kids in the family and had a huge grocery bill every week. My mother could call them and not have to worry about it. We got about 20 to 25 bags of groceries every week. We had milk delivered by Oberlin Farms, and a fruit guy, Tony, came to the house, too. He had a truck full of fruit—peaches, cherries, apples, and black raspberries, which made my favorite pie.
> – *Dennis King, Rocky River*

> There was a guy who drove a truck very slowly down our street on summer mornings, calling out what sounded like "Paper Eggs." I know he sold eggs, but I'm not sure what the "Paper" was all about. Our corner grocery store also delivered to the house. My mom or grandmother would send me or my sister up to the store with the grocery list, and a boy would bring the order in a box later that day. Charlie's Chips used to be delivered, too. Thus began a dangerous, lifelong love affair between me and potato chips. – *Carol Lally Metz, Cleveland (East Side)*

LET THE CHIPS FALL

Charles Chips have been around since 1942. Their brown-and-tan can was a point of distinction, and so was the fact that they were delivered right to your door.

> On one street—a typical suburban University Heights grid neighborhood—probably 16 out of 24 houses had Charles Chips delivered, and 20 of 24 had milk and cottage cheese delivered. – *Steve Presser Cleveland Heights/University Heights*

> Charles Chips brought us chips, pretzels, and peanut brittle. – *Eileen Murray, North Olmsted*

GROCERY-GRAM: for folks who didn't drive, grocery stores delivered food right to the door.

YUM-YUM: Num-Num Potato Chips, Pretzel Sticks, and French Fried Popcorn came from the Noss Pretzel Company on Lorain Avenue.

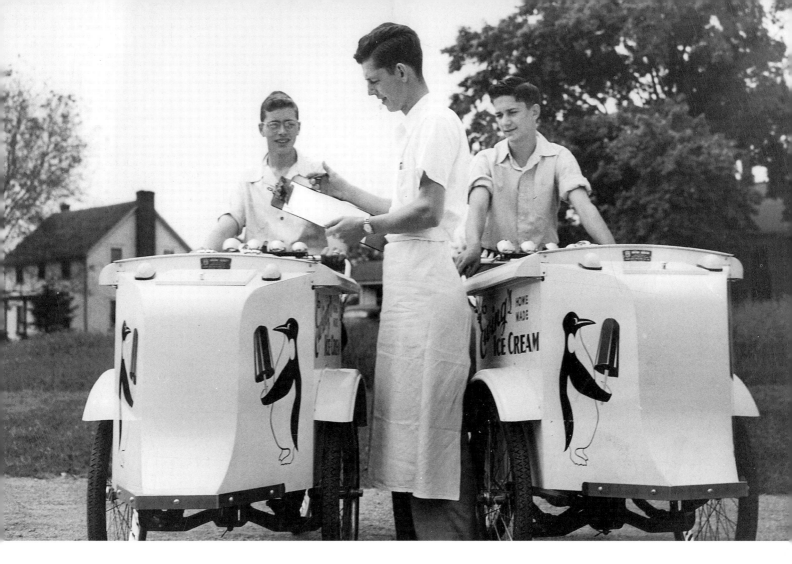

ICE-CREAM PEDDLERS: in the 1950s, kids in Rocky River looked for Ewing Ice Cream carts to turn onto their streets.

We had Charles Chips come to the house for pretzels and potato chips. The potato chips were my favorite by far. They came in a big can, so you got a lot more.
– *Dennis King*

Charles Chips were uniformly dark, darker than most chips you could buy, and they were just salty enough. – *Pat Fernberg*

ICE CREAM

The coolest delivered foods were undoubtedly the things that arrived with the ice-cream man.

That was the one song we all heard—that ice-cream truck tune, turning the corner. We all ran out of the house . . . If you were a big shot, you could treat your friend for a quarter, or 50 cents. – *Steve Presser*

I remember the Popsicle man, and getting Eskimo Pies from him. But one time, all he had left were root beer–flavored Popsicles. He gave them to us. We thought we were getting a really good deal, but they were nasty. We didn't like them.
– *Susanne Apple, Macedonia*

MILK

Those who remember the name of the milk company that delivered their family's milk often remember the milkman's name, and what the family ordered, as well. The names include Producer's, Dairymen's, Belle Vernon, Dean's, Hillside, Myers, Moss Dairy, Old Meadow, and more. Some families stayed with the same dairy for 50 years.

One Clevelander remembers not only the Euclid Race Dairy trucks that drove around his neighborhood, but also recalls stopping in for ice cream at their locations on Grovewood and at East 200th Street.

> At the counter under the cash register, there was an animated cow that looked like it had fur on it. When you're about three years old, it's pretty cool. It nodded its head and swung its tail.
>
> – *Joe Valencic, Cleveland (North Collinwood/Beachland)*

> Milk was plentiful. The milkman brought it to the house in the horse and buggy. It was always one buttermilk, and one sweet milk with the cream on it. But you'd better not run with it and shake it up. My momma always got that for her coffee. That was our favorite part of milk until they started homogenizing it.
>
> – *Robert McAlpine, Cleveland (East 55th St.)*

CHANGE IN RETAIL PRICES
Effective August 1, 1936

	Quarts	Pints	½ Pints
Regular Milk			
Class "1" Milk	.12	.07	
Guernsey Milk	.14	.08	
Table Cream	.15	.09	
Whipping Cream	.56	.30	.15
Sour Cream	.74	.42	.21
Buttermilk—Old Fashioned Churned	.56	.30	.15
Chocolate Milk	.09	.05	
Cottage Cheese, Creamed	.14	.08	

12-oz. container, 13c each

Blain Dairies Inc.
PASTEURIZED

17425 Lorain Av   CLEVELAND 2, O.

"LOCAL   ter 1605

IN ACCOUNT WITH
LIBERTY DAIRY
MILK and CREAM
3338 W. 52nd ST.   WOodbine 2353

Bal. Brought Forward	
PTS. MILK	
QTS. MILK	
QTS. HOMOGENIZED V.D. MILK	
QTS. CHOCOLATE MILK	
QTS. BUTTERMILK	
½ PTS. SWEET CREAM	
PTS. SWEET CREAM	
½ PTS. SOUR CREAM	
PTS. SOUR CREAM	
½ PTS. WHIPPING CREAM	
PTS. WHIPPING CREAM	
CHEESE	

RECEIVED PAYMENT   M. OTRHALIK & SON
DATE   PER

DAIRY AT YOUR DOOR: you'd think the milkman arrived too early to get to know customers, but that wasn't the case. More often than not, folks were on a first-name basis with the driver who left their order in the milk chute, on the porch, or by the side door.

MILKING IT: Hillside Dairy was just one of many companies that made the milk appear at our doors.

PRICE CHECK

1932: A quart of milk sold for 8 cents at the Buckeye Heights Creamery & Delicatessen, 12526 Buckeye Road.

1967: A gallon of Sealtest Milk was 81 cents at Murman's, 19525 Hilliard Road, Rocky River.

1968: A half-gallon of Lockie Lee 2 percent milk sold for 39 cents at Convenient Food Mart, 18212 Sloan Avenue, Lakewood.

Steve Presser, who grew up in University Heights, remembers the milkman with fondness. "George the milkman was just a wonderful, wonderful man whom all of the kids in the neighborhood loved. He was the driver for pretty much our entire childhood." Presser wasn't the only kid who knew the milkman on a first-name basis, either.

We got milk and eggs from Hillside. Bud was our carrier.
– *Sali A. McSherry, Chagrin Falls*

Moss Dairy delivered the milk to our milk chute.
– *Linda Goodman Robiner, University Heights*

Our milk was delivered by Producer's. The milk, which came in brown bottles, was cold and delicious. Milk just doesn't taste the same these days. – *Eileen Murray*

We had Dairymen's milk and eggs delivered. Sometime he would bring orange juice, but that was rare. – *Dorothy Bell, Cleveland (Near East Side)*

BAKED GOODS

For those who wanted them, products like coffee cake or bread could arrive on wheels too.

I'll never forget nearly laughing myself silly with my cousins and sisters when the guy who delivered baked goods to my aunt's house in Lakewood went over every ingredient in what had to have been the worst fruitcake we'd ever tasted . . . "all your

Citroen peels—orange, lemon and lime." Gee, my junior high school French teacher used to drive one of those cars, but this was the first time I'd ever heard of one being peeled for a fruitcake! – *George Ghetia, Lakewood*

AND EVEN MORE ARRIVING AT THE DOOR

Once people got into the swing of things, it seems they found an almost endless array of food and drink that could be brought right to the door.

As a child, I remember a guy with his white, sway-backed horse bringing the cart with fruits and vegetables down the street. I was most interested in the horse. – *Pat Fernberg*

My mother had chicken delivered from a kosher chicken store on Coventry in Cleveland Heights. You would call up, and they would kill the chicken at the store, de-feather it, and deliver it to the house. My mother always had it delivered to the house, once a week on Thursday, for the Jewish sabbath on Friday and Saturday. – *Helen Weinberger*

We got our coffee from Cook's Coffee Company. We also used to purchase a cheese-cake mix from them. – *Eileen Murray*

FIZZY STUFF IN THE FLATS: Coca-Cola was invented in 1886 as a soda fountain beverage that sold for 5 cents a glass. By 1905, there was a bottling plant in Cleveland, and the bottler had three horse-drawn wagons in the Flats.

The Sweet Stuff

For years you probably obeyed your mom's edict to clean your plate before you dashed outside to intercept the Good Humor ice-cream truck. No doubt she also told you to avoid eating cookie dough or swallowing your bubble gum. Times have changed. Now you can buy raw cookie dough or bubble gum in your ice cream, and you're old enough to eat it anytime you want.

For baby boomers around the country, Pez candy, Eskimo Pies, and those Hostess Cupcakes advertised on the *Howdy Doody Show* probably summon childhood memories. But the fact is that those things are a blast from a more distant culinary past. Pez arrived on the scene in 1927, while Eskimo Pies and Hostess Cupcakes have been smearing kids' faces since 1919.

"THE BIRD" WAS THE WORD: Penguin Frozen Custard was worth the ride to Fairview Park.

Here in Cleveland, our contemporary sweet memories may involve the Euclid Race Dairy mechanical cow at the counter, or Laughing Sal, that scary mechanical gal we watched at Euclid Beach while eating our Humphrey Candy Kisses. Wherever we bought them, ice cream and candy were important parts of our childhood, and there's no evidence that they spoiled our dinner. No evidence at all.

ICE-CREAM DREAMS

Weber's, Penguin, Boukair's, Draeger's, Malley's, Dairy Queen, Dairy King, Meither's, Franklin's, Isaly's, Euclid Beach Frozen Whip . . . the list goes on and on. Don't get into an argument with a Clevelander about the best place to go for ice cream, because there's not just one right answer. The simple truth is, it might not have been as much the taste of ice cream as it was the romance of the place, or the sweet aftertaste of memory.

Ice cream is a cool idea that may have originated in ancient times when people used snow and honey as a base, but we've definitely improved on it. We've even built stands and stores devoted to it. For some folks, the decor played a major role in their ice-cream experience.

ICE-CREAM ACCESSORIES: items such as the Producers Milk ice-cream bowl and wooden spoon made the ice-cream experience seem more tasty.

COOL DEAL: Franklin Ice Cream sold specialties such as Toasted Almond Fudge Cake Rolls and party slices, and dispensed wooden spoons to eat them with.

Without a doubt, without exception, and without hesitation, Malley's in Lakewood was my favorite place to go for ice cream. My sisters and brothers even appeared in a print ad for Father's Day. They are depicted giving their dad a box of Malley's chocolates. Up until the mid-'80s, the interior of Malley's was decorated in an odd way. Done up in pink and green, the walls of the ice-cream parlor area featured ice-cream tables and sheer curtains, and on the walls hung what can only be described as the trophy heads of carousel animals—honestly. It was like being in Bozo the Clown's den. In addition to being slightly scary on their own, the heads were hung at the right angle for adults, but if you were a kid, they were just too high up on the wall, the unicorns and horses peering down at you with imposing looks. Sometime in the 1980s, Malley's redecorated with an Alice in Wonderland theme, which is much more palatable, and a bit less kitschy for my tastes. Malley's sundaes are served with a plate of thin, salty pretzels. Nowhere else in the country have I ever experienced pretzels with ice cream. If you tell out-of-towners about it, they think you're a little crazy. – *Miriam Carey, Cleveland*

"It was like being in Bozo the Clown's den."

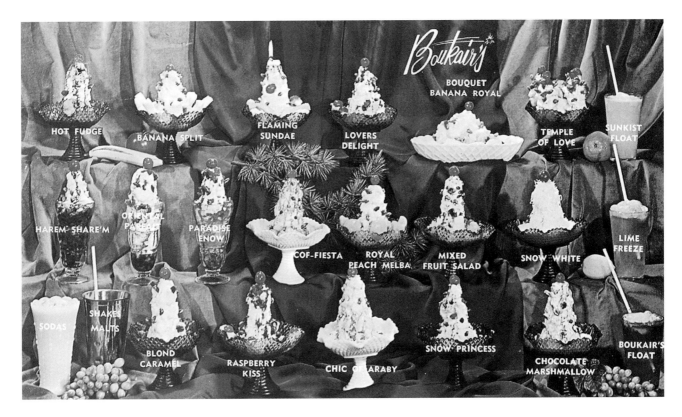

GETTING IN OUR LICKS: whether it came to us on the Good Humor truck or we went after it at places like Boukair's, ice cream had drawing power.

Boukair's SeeSweets at Playhouse Square had a romance all its own, ranging from the glitzy interior to the bright-pink menu cover. Inside the menu, the romantically named sundaes were illustrated in color. Moe Boukair gave the ice-cream creations such coolly exotic names as Chic of Araby, Harem Share 'Em, Temple of Love, and Raspberry Kiss. It was the interior of Boukair's at Playhouse Square, though, that left a lasting impression on one Clevelander. "I remember the ambiance. It was all done in pastel colors, with drop-down lights of the shape you see in a lava lamp. It was very bright, and very cool looking," says Gary Grabowski.

Some people tend to be sentimental about their children's first ice-cream experiences, and about continuing family traditions. Angela Wilkes grew up in Georgia but says the Cleveland food spot that has made the greatest impression on her family is Draeger's Ice Cream in Shaker Heights, because that's the place where her son had his first ice-cream cone. Native Clevelander Sam DeGaetano has another ice-cream memory: "Hoffman's Ice Cream on Euclid, next to the Alhambra Theatre, was a hangout when I was in high school. They did burgers and fries, and made the greatest ice-cream sundaes in the world."

COOL STUFF AT EUCLID BEACH

For some at Euclid Beach Park (1901–1969), the rides were a rite of summer, but for many, the munchies were the stuff of memories. Euclid Beach was owned and operated by the Humphrey family. On the menu: the Humphreys' specially grown hull-less popcorn, hot dogs sold at the Colonnade lunch stand, and that cool, creamy Frozen Whip.

The Frozen Whip at Euclid Beach Park was as much a signature as the automated figure of Laughing Sal, the funhouse gal who rocked with laughter to entice visitors. The food at the amusement park was as memorable as rides like Over the Falls, Flying Turns, and the Rocket Ships.

> In the 1950s, we lived at 105th and St. Clair and had to take two buses to Euclid Beach. We only went once in a while, because we didn't have a car. I couldn't sleep the night before because I would think about what I was going to eat: Humphrey Popcorn Balls and candy kisses. Mainly, what I liked more than anything was hot

QUEEN FOR A DAY: a hot-weather rush and a 1-cent sale brought 'em out to the Dairy Queen at West 58th and Memphis in 1959.

dogs. They were delicious and we didn't have them at home because my mother kept kosher. I ate about four hot dogs, and then had frozen custard, and candy kisses and popcorn balls. Once, in the summertime coming home on the bus, I got sick and threw up on the bus, and my father yelled at me. I didn't eat hot dogs for 30 years after that. – *Helen Weinberger*

At Miracles, we served what we called "Euclid Beach Style" frozen custard. We had a customer who wanted to talk with me about the frozen custard. Her father had been the man who built the equipment to make it, and she gave ours the stamp of approval. At Euclid Beach, it used to fly down the chute and get paddled into the cone. – *Rita M. Grabowski, co-owner (with husband Gary Grabowski) of the now-closed Miracles restaurant in Tremont*

AN EPIDEMIC OF ICE-CREAM MOUSTACHES

While there's no official evidence that Clevelanders had anything to do with inventing the milk moustache, we can sure lay claim to the Frosty Moustache. We earned them at the Frosty Bar in the Higbee's and May Company basements. The milk shake was sometimes as hard to drink as it was delicious, because it didn't come with a spoon.

> The Frosty's in Higbee's and the May Company was a chocolate-milk drink something like Wendy's produces today. You'd step up to the counter, have a Frosty, and continue shopping. – *Therese Hummer, Cleveland*

> One of my favorite food memories is the malted at Higbee's, so thick that you had a moustache when you drank it. – *Helen Weinberger*

> I remember getting Frosty ice-cream moustaches in the basement of Higbee's. We stopped there on our way to the Rapid. – *David Farkas, Cleveland*

> For a birthday present, my grandmother used to take her grandchildren downtown to shop and eat. We'd go to Higbee's for clothes and eat in their restaurant, often ordering their special kids' lunch served in a small stove. Then we'd stop for one of their malted milk drinks, which were totally delicious. I remember the drink stand was under an escalator. – *Carol Lally Metz*

DRUGSTORE SODA FOUNTAIN

When Anne Kwait and her late husband, pharmacist Nate Kwait, took over Webb Pharmacy on Detroit Avenue in Lakewood, the soda fountain was already in place. Kwait recalls:

> At first we just served ice cream and all the Coke or root beer you could drink for a nickel. We made our own simple syrup and our own chocolate syrup. We boiled it on

The milk shake was sometimes as hard to drink as it was delicious, because it didn't come with a spoon.

a hotplate in the back of the drugstore. We enlarged the soda fountain in 1936 or 1937—we broke through a wall and made it bigger with booths. There were eight counter stools, and three booths. Next we put in a grill, and then we offered sandwiches. We had ice cream in five-pound cartons, and we hand-packed it for people who wanted to buy it to take it home. The Coke dispenser had a pull-down handle, and we had two sizes of Coke glasses.

Stephen G. Michaelides, who grew up in Cleveland Heights in the 1940s and 1950s, worked at the soda fountain of Uberstine's Drug Store on the corner of Coventry and Mayfield, but he also recalls another favorite spot from the 1940s: "There was a wonderful ice-cream place on Lee Road that we used to hit in high school. It was Meither's."

DAIRY QUEEN

It was in 1940 that Dairy Queen first started serving its cones with a signature curlicue on top of the ice cream. That was in Joliet, Illinois. By the 1950s, Clevelanders got in on the fun, especially those who lived within a few blocks of a Dairy Queen.

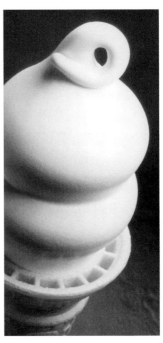

> That changed everybody's evening pattern right away. All of a sudden, everybody walked over there and got Dairy Queen stuff in the summertime.
> – Bob Krummert, Cleveland (West Park)

> We had a very early Dairy Queen on Memphis Road. No cakes in the freezer; they just handed the cones out through the window.
> – Rita M. Grabowski

ISALY'S

Isaly's started in 1931 in Pittsburgh. The company opened a store in Berea, Ohio, that operated from 1940 to 1965. In the 1950s, more than 400 Isaly's stores were operating, mostly in Ohio and Pennsylvania. By the 1960s, Clevelanders were getting in their licks at numerous locations, including those in Bedford, Brookpark, Garfield Heights, Independence, Maple Heights, Mayfield and Mayfield Heights, Parkview, Chagrin Falls, Chardon, Solon, Parma, Painesville, and Willoughby.

Many deli and dairy fans recall Isaly's ice-cream shops. In 1996, Klondike bars made the grade as the best-selling ice-cream novelty in the U.S. For years, though, only those of us living in Ohio and in the Pittsburgh area were lucky enough to be able to bite into those rich, chocolate-covered ice-cream bars sold in Isaly's. In the 1960s, Klondikes were selling for 28 cents each.

CONE HEADS: when places like Isaly's or Dairy Queen opened up in Cleveland-area neighborhoods, it was big, cool news.

Stephen Michaelides says Isaly's is one of the places he'd like to bring back. In particular, he remembers its thick-rimmed coffee cups.

NUTS ABOUT NUTS

A sundae without nuts is like a ball game without peanuts. Peterson Nut Company (6133 Rockside Road) has been putting crunch into our lives since 1927, but we also satisfied our cravings at drugstores, department stores, and elsewhere. A West Sider and an East Sider share some summertime memories.

When I worked summers as a deputy clerk for probate court, I went to Morrow's Nut House on Euclid Avenue at lunch. We'd eat so many red pistachios that we'd go back to probate court with red dye all over our lips. We must have looked like rodeo clowns. – *Bob Krummert*

I used to go down to the ball games and sell peanuts. I put about 10 peanuts in a bag and sold them–four bags for a dollar. I was 13 or 14. I got a lot of business; I always sold out. – *Robert McAlpine*

THE SCOOP ON ICE-CREAM TERMINOLOGY

You may remember having the Frozen Whip sold at Euclid Beach Park, stopping at the Frosty Bar in the Higbee Company, or buying an ice-cream cone at your favorite neighborhood soda fountain and seeing an advertisement that you were being served French Ice Cream. But did you really know what that was? Here are some definitions.

FRENCH ICE CREAM AND FROZEN CUSTARD: These must contain at least 10 percent milk fat, as well as at least 1.4 percent egg yolk solids. Premium custard, however, may not contain egg yolks. Anne Kwait recalls that French ice cream was served at Webb Pharmacy in Lakewood in the 1940s and 1950s: "We served Pierre's French Ice Cream—vanilla, chocolate, butter pecan, strawberry and cherry vanilla."

GELATO: Italian ice cream that has a denser texture than the American version, due to the fact that it contains less air. It's made with sweeteners, dairy products, egg yolks, and flavoring. You can find it at such local places as La Gelateria, 12421 Cedar Road.

ICE CREAM: It's made of milk products and sweetener, plus it sometimes contains solid additions such as cookies, fruit, chocolate, or even bubble gum. In the U.S. ice cream has to be at least 10 percent milk fat unless it has solid additions, in which case it must contain at least 8 percent milk fat.

ICE/GRANITÉ/GRANITA: Depending on whether you're in the U.S., France, or Italy, you'll have a different name for this frozen mixture of water, sugar, and liquid flavoring such as coffee or fruit juice. It's usually a mixture of four parts liquid to one part sugar.

ICE MILK: Contains less milk solids and less milk fat. Maybe you bought some at Lawson's.

SHERBET: This has its roots in charbet, a Middle Eastern beverage made with sweetened fruit juice and water. Sherbet may also contain milk (1 percent to 2 percent), gelatin, or egg whites.

SORBET: It's similar to sherbet, but without the dairy products.

CANDY

Making candy can be an exasperating—or exhilarating—experience. Jodi Kanter, who grew up in Lyndhurst in the 1960s, notes, "I first learned to cook out of a Girl Scout cookbook. I made candy; I was 10." Most of us weren't quite that ambitious. We bought our candy, and were willing to go out of our way to do so.

Ellie Yanky grew up in the '70s in Berea, and has fond candy recollections from childhood:

> As soon as we got into kindergarten, we'd ride our bikes with the older kids down to Spafford's in Berea for penny candy. We'd buy enough to fill a lunch-bag type of paper bag. I liked the candy dots on paper, Tootsie Pops, bubble gum with baseball cards, and reading the Bazooka Joe comics and fortunes that came with the bubble gum. I also got the jawbreakers with layers that turned different colors. You'd have to keep taking it out of your mouth to check to see what color it was.

Steve Presser, who refers to himself as the "Big Cheese" of Big Fun (the nostalgia toy store on Coventry Road) and Dottie's Diner (on Lee Road) in Cleveland Heights, was drawn by the visual appeal of retro candy in the 1950s and 1960s, and liked "anything that would make a dentist squeal." He recalls that he even got into competitive candy-eating:

> I liked Jawbreakers, and Bonomo's Turkish Taffy was probably my favorite. I called it "the pink flavor" when I was a kid—strawberry. It liked it to be hard enough to crack, but soft enough to chew. Also, I am unbeaten at eating the colored dots on paper. I have a technique where you wrap your finger around it. It's like eating corn. Growing up, we had contests: You couldn't eat too much paper, and you couldn't tear it, and you had to eat it all. I am undefeated at candy dots eating.

> My favorite gum was Fan Tan, which we bought after dinner at the counter in the Chinese Garden Restaurant.
> – *Laurie Orr, Lakewood*

"I remember trips to Euclid Beach," says Bob Krummert, who grew up in Cleveland's West Park neighborhood in the 1950s. "Not to Euclid Beach Park, per se, but going all the

CHAT AND CHEW: never let it be said that Clevelanders couldn't talk and chew gum at the same time. Sometimes we even did the Teaberry Shuffle while we were chewing it.

CANDY LAND: some types of candy and gum could only be found at the corner store, a movie theater, or a vending machine at your favorite diner.

way out there just to get bags and bags of candy kisses on a hot summer night. That was a long way before Interstate 90. It took a long time to get there by car. We went all that way for the kisses, that's how much we liked them. We went to the little stand up front."

POP CULTURE

No, we're not talking about Andy Warhol's 1962 painting *Green Coca-Cola Bottles*. Clevelanders were guzzling soft drinks long before that. But it is true that Coke machines had their own allure, as did the small bottles of Coca-Cola that came out of them. Cleveland native Mark Lewine remembers, "The ice-cold 8-ounce bottle of Coke coming down that red machine . . . nothing will replace that for me."

"Soft drink" is kind of a stuffy name. Whether you called it "pop," "soda pop," or simply "soda" largely depends on the part of the country where you grew up. Cleveland is "pop" territory. That's how we refer generically to stuff like root beer. A root beer soda is something else entirely, something with ice cream in it and a dollop of whipped cream on top. Your cousins living elsewhere in the country might have disagreed with your terminology, but then, they were out there calling submarine sandwiches stuff like "grinders" and "po'boys," too.

LITTLE PACKAGES: Little Tom ("The Best Things Come in Little Packages") Bottling Company of Cleveland sold kid-pleasing six-ounce pop bottles.

You can thank Cleveland chemist Graham W. Clarke for figuring out how to liquefy carbonic acid gas, because he made it possible for the soft drink industry (oops—make that the pop industry) to develop. Fizzy favorites didn't have to come in a bottle, either. By the 1940s, soda jerks were filling up a lot of glasses with freshly made phosphates. These fountain drinks combined flavored syrup and seltzer water. Chocolate, vanilla, and cherry phosphates were big favorites.

Beverage stores sold small bottles of soda, such as O-So and Little Tom—soft drinks that offered kid-sized portions and created a feeling of plenty. The bottles were small enough that kids could finish them and go back for more. Dennis King, who grew up in Rocky River in the 1960s, recollects a typical O-So occasion. "The big thing at First Communions was having O-So's and cake. I'd have about 12 bottles of O-So, except I didn't like the cream soda. My favorite was root beer, or black cherry."

Cleveland is "pop" territory.

FRESH FROM THE BAKERY

The alluring aromas, flavors, and taste traditions of bakery products are among our fondest food memories. All across the city, people were likely to close their eyes, as if they were anticipating a kiss, when they bit into rich specialties like cream puffs and chocolate éclairs. En route to the Rapid after work, we stopped at a bakery on the lower level of the Terminal Tower for a Boston Cream Pie. Some of us dropped into Lucy's on Buckeye Road for strudel. Downtown workers stopped on their lunch hour to pick up an apple pie at the Colonnade. And after doing the rest of her grocery shopping, many a mom dashed next door to the bakery for a cinnamon walnut coffee cake for the next morning's breakfast.

> My dad worked in the city, and we lived in Brunswick. He would bring home bagels, cassata cake, and other things our neighbors had never heard of. He brought bagels to Brunswick. For my parents' wedding anniversary on St. Patrick's Day (they were Lithuanian), he would always buy Italian cassata cake and one green carnation for every year they had been married. The neighbors would drop over because they knew we'd have cassata cake. That's part of being American. We get the best to choose from. To this day, when I travel I always make it a point to go to local markets. It's almost like being an anthropologist. How do you know what people are like if you don't know what they eat? – *Lyn Byrd*

> We lived directly across from Kelly Donuts in Lakewood, and you'd wake up to the smell of fresh doughnuts every morning, which is a fabulous thing. We knew everybody there by first name. It was like an old-fashioned bakery, where they took pride in their products. Their doughnuts were very much the old-fashioned, yeast-raised type. The maple cream was so sweet it could put you into sugar shock. – *Pat Fernberg*

CASE WORKERS: whether we wanted bread, cookies, or pastries, our favorite bakeries were staffed with people who could supply them.

CAKE WALK: customers lined up outside Hough Bakery in 1945 after the V-J Day holiday. At other times, storks in the stores reminded us that cakes were great for baby showers and christenings.

Fairview Bakery, on Lorain Road, was the source of our bread and incredible glazed donuts. – *Eileen Murray*

At Lucy's on Buckeye, I still get good Hungarian bakery, in a neighborhood with hardly any Hungarians left. – *Mark Lewine*

CAKE DECO: putting on the finishing touches that made Hough Bakery cakes so popular are (left to right) Robert Pile, Kenneth Pile, John Odoski, Lawrence Pile, and Arthur Pile in 1945.

WHICH ONE IS THE VANILLA ANNIVERSARY? Hough Bakeries commemorative plates celebrate the company's fiftieth and seventy-fifth anniversaries.

Anna Chenin is a certified executive pastry chef, and spent 55 years working in the baking industry. She has studied pastry arts at the Culinary Institute of America, at Johnson and Wales University, and in Paris. As a baking chef, she also taught for 18 years at Cuyahoga Community College. But it all began when she was 15 years old.

"I worked for New York Bakery for 28 years. At one time, it was on Mayfield Road. We started out at 91st and St. Clair. I was going to high school and was working at the bakery. I loved the decorating. It really took me. I'll tell you, I did that for the rest of my life. I really enjoyed it." She continues, "When I was in it, I was the only woman. There were only a few women certified."

Anne Kwait recalls some of her all-time favorite bakery products: "At Kaase's Bakery, near Warren Road in Lakewood, I bought kuchen. And my favorite was whipped cream puffs and éclairs with French crème inside them."

Patricia Demski, a native of the Brooklyn area of Cleveland, graduated from the Culinary Institute of America in Hyde Park, New York, and is a pastry chef. "If Hough Bakery would open again," she says, "I think they'd do a wonderful business."

"Who wants a fungus pie?"

And she's not alone. It's hard to imagine any closed Cleveland establishment being mourned more than Hough Bakery. Their cakes didn't merely taste good, they were symbols of specialness consumed at important events like birthdays, weddings, retirement parties, and holidays. T. S. Eliot, in his poem "The Love Song of J. Alfred Prufrock," talks about measuring out a life with coffee spoons, but it seems that Clevelanders have instead measured out their lives in cakes from Hough Bakery.

In our collective memory, those creations were to cake what a down comforter is to an old army blanket. As we remember them, the cakes were softer, sweeter, and more satisfying than most. Some say they had a flavor of almond; others credit an extra jolt of sugar.

Online at the Uncle Phaedrus Consulting Detective and Finder of Lost Recipes website (www.hungrybrowser.com/phaedrus), you'll see a list of the detective's "cold cases." Number five on that national list is requests for recipes from Hough Bakery. A note at the site says, "None, I repeat, absolutely none, of Hough Bakery's recipes have made it online."

> Why, oh why, won't someone bring back Hough Bakery? Sure, everyone remembers the cheese crown Danish, the cookies, and the "usual suspects" from Hough, but we had a secret weapon to order from our favorite bakery: The Mushroom Pie. Our garage was set far back from the house, so when my dad would come home from work, we would watch through the kitchen window as he approached the house. If he had that signature blue-and-white, string-tied box in his hands, we'd start salivating for Hough Bakery.
>
> More often than not, though, there were two mushroom pies inside those boxes. At first, this was a big disappointment. Who wants a fungus pie? But this odd delicacy soon grew on us and became a staple at fancy family meals. Hough's pie crusts were flaky, buttery, and brown, and I cannot replicate them in my kitchen. The Mushroom Pie was nothing but mushrooms sauteed in butter and flavored slightly with salt and pepper. Something must have held it together; perhaps there was an egg base, but the pies never seemed eggy. Try as we might, we can't come up with a recipe that approximates this delicious treat, so please, someone, dig up the old Hough files. – *Miriam Carey*

Hough Bakery was founded in 1903 by Lionel Pile. By 1973, the company had grown to 1,000 employees.

> From 1954 to 1955, I worked at Hough Bakery at Cedar-Fairmount. I remember learning how to tie up the boxes with bakery string. You could cut your fingers on it. I learned the names of all kinds of rolls and cookies. I always had a passion for after-dinner mints, and when no one was looking, you could snatch a few. – *Sheila Bellamy, Cleveland Heights*

Just about everybody remembers a particular product from Hough Bakery: coffee cakes, brownies, hot cross buns, dinner rolls, mints, petits fours, glazed doughnuts, and more. A recollection by Clevelander Joe Valencic adds to the mystique. "Coconut chocolate bars are thought to have been invented in Cleveland, and were popularized by Hough Bakeries—bars of pound cake dipped in chocolate sauce and rolled in finely chopped coconut."

Steve Presser's favorite was the white-on-white cake; he always chose the piece with the most flowers. Clevelanders even feel nostalgic about the nonedible remnants of the legendary bakery. Presser explains that people who collect local food memorabilia have a special fondness for Hough Bakery because it was such an important part of people's lives.

HATS OFF: just the sight of hats or trays from Hough Bakeries can summon taste memories of birthday cakes, petits fours, mints, and other treats.

Bread Alone

James Beard, the dean of American cooking, called good bread with fresh butter the greatest of feasts, and few people would argue with that. When our ancestors came to Cleveland, they brought their breads—and their taste in bread—with them. Eventually, though, we all began taking bites out of each other's culinary heritage. Today, we find challah, ciabatta, pitas, and tortillas comingling on our supermarket shelves.

When the commercial bread slicer was invented in 1928, toasters were not far behind. In 1939, 66 percent of the bread consumed in the U.S. was commercially baked. By 1945, that figure had risen to 85 percent. Although many of us think of Wonder Bread as being a 1950s invention, the truth is that the Continental Baking Company introduced it in 1927, and began selling sliced loaves in 1930. Here are some bread memories.

SOUND BITE

Bread in its many variations can be seen as an expression of ethnicity, identity, or national pride. It's said that contemporary French chefs are advising the country's young people to "listen to their bread." That, of course, refers to the fact that crusty traditional breads made in the artisan tradition create a sound when one bites into them, whereas the cottony fast-food burger buns do not.

> I remember my grandmother's Irish soda bread. Actually, I remember all of her breads, but I later found out she didn't bake them. She bought them, and then sliced them and put them in the bread box. My grandfather was a driver for Fisher's. I think that's where the bread came from. Somebody in the family once saw the bread in a Fisher's bag and said to her, "Hey, you didn't bake that bread—you bought it." My grandmother answered, "Never you mind. It's my bread." But when I once mentioned to a relative that I missed my grandmother's bread, the Irish soda bread and the other kinds, I was told she didn't bake those other kinds of bread. *– Katie Smith, Parma Heights*

THE GREATEST THING: sliced or unsliced, with caraway seeds or without, there's nothing like a fresh loaf of bread.

BETTER BREAD: everybody's mom had a favorite brand of bread.

We ate Wonder Bread on a daily basis, but since my dad worked in the city, he'd sometimes bring home good rye bread from the Central Market. – Lyn Byrd

We must have come home with an occasional loaf of rye or Vienna from the West Side Market, but I rarely remember eating much besides Wonder Bread as a kid. In sixth grade, I went home with a classmate and walked through the door just as her mother had taken a loaf of Italian bread out of the oven. That transformed my concept of bread. – Rita M. Grabowski

My mother made the bread we ate. My father said store bread wasn't fit to eat, because you could roll it up into a ball. – Janice Orr

We probably ate Tip Top. I used to run to the Shaker Market at the corner to buy bread. – Karen Perry

I was fascinated when they started selling sliced bread. I called it light bread. Some people called it white bread. I used to go by the bakery, Hough Bakery, and they'd give us the ends. The bakery was on Lakeview Avenue.
– Robert McAlpine

Every Sunday we'd go to church, and then to Alesci's at Great Northern. They always had a lot of fresh-baked breads. When we'd go there, they'd be taking that Italian bread out of the oven. You couldn't cut it until it got to a certain temperature, but you always wanted the fresh bread. So you'd sit there and wait and wait and wait until it got to the right temperature. Then they'd put the bread on the slicer and slice it up. You'd put it into the bag, and it would still be warm.

   I always got yelled at, because from the time we went from the store to the time we'd get home, I ate half the loaf of bread. My dad would be in the front saying, "Quit eating the bread," and I'd say, "I'm not eating the bread." What it evolved into was that we wound up buying two loaves of bread. I loved Alesci's. There were good food memories there. *– Michael Symon, North Olmsted*

One food memory I have is of a bakery we'd go to on the West Side. We would time it perfectly, so the bread was coming out of the oven, and we'd pick it up to take to my grandmother's house. We'd buy three loaves: two loaves for the family, and one that never made it. We'd bust it up in the car—it was so hot you could barely hold on to it—and it was one of the great food memories I have. I believe the bakery is still around, in the West 47th and Lorain Avenue area. It's funny because when you're a kid you think of eating sweet chocolate, but one of my memories is eating bread, Italian bread. *– Michael Sanson, Bay Village*

KNEADY PEOPLE: bakers at Alesci's turned out the stuff of which memories were made.

CRUST AND CULTURE

The variety of breads defined in *The New Food Lover's Companion* illustrates how the staff of life is linked to Cleveland culture through the city's various ethnic groups.

POLISH: Babka—rum-scented sweet yeast bread

FRENCH: Brioche—yeast bread made with butter and eggs; French bread—crusty, light yeast bread made with water instead of milk

ITALIAN: Bruschetta—traditional garlic bread, toasted and rubbed with garlic; Focaccia—round, flat bread drizzled with olive oil, salt, and rosemary

JEWISH: Challah—yeast bread served on the Sabbath

BRITISH: Crumpets—yeast-raised bread (the size of English muffins) made of unsweetened batter cooked on a stovetop griddle

SCANDINAVIAN: Flat bread—thin, cracker-like bread made with rye flour

NAVAJO AND HOPI: Fry bread—deep-fried bread made of flour, water, and salt

IRISH: Soda bread—quick bread that uses soda as its leavening; a cross is slashed into the top of the loaf before baking

MIDDLE EASTERN: Lahvosh—also known as Armenian cracker bread, it is round, thin, and crisp; Pita—a round pocket bread

EAST INDIAN: Naan bread—lightly leavened with yeast, baked in a tandoor oven; Paratha—flaky bread made from whole-wheat flour, fried on a griddle; Chapati—unleavened pancake-like griddle bread of whole-wheat flour and water

INDIAN AND PAKISTANI: Poori—deep-fried unleavened bread made with whole-wheat flour, water, and ghee (clarified butter)

SCOTTISH: Scone—quick bread originally griddle-baked and made with oats

MEXICAN: Tortilla—unleavened pancake-style bread made of masa or wheat flour, baked on a griddle

GERMAN: Zwieback—twice-baked sweetened bread that's cut into slices

PRICE CHECK

1925: A loaf of fresh-baked "Grandmother's Bread" sold for 10 cents at the A & P on East 30th Street in Cleveland.

1934: A loaf of rye or Vienna bread sold for 6 cents at Pavny's, 12526 Buckeye Road.

1956: You could get two one-pound loaves of sliced white bread for 29 cents at Cleveland-area Kroger stores.

1968: Two loaves of bread were still available for 29 cents at Convenient Food Mart, West 220th and Lorain in Fairview Park, and 18212 Sloan Avenue in Lakewood, as part of a special sale.

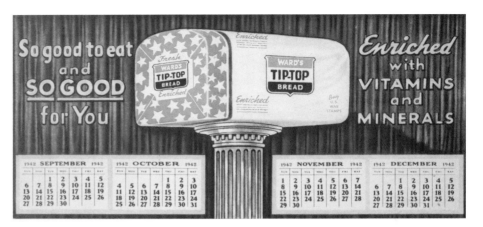

WARD'S TO THE WISE: in the 1940s, Ward's Tip-Top Bread blotters advised customers to "Buy U.S. War Stamps."

Made in Cleveland

Homegrown produce, good old tap water from Lake Erie, maple syrup from Geauga County, and products made right here at home seem to have a special taste all their own.

Chef/owner Michael Symon of Lola in Tremont says we're known for our mustard and for Eastern European influences in our food. "I think Northeast Ohio food is predominantly Eastern European in influence. People outside of Cleveland know us for pierogies, fish frys—which are a very Eastern European thing—and bratwurst."

Our wealth of food products doesn't stop there, though. As Cleveland native Joe Valencic notes, the area has a tasty history of food production.

> People went into town for food, but they also went out of town, to Lake County to pick their own apples, or to Amish country. When the Ohio Canal opened, Cleveland was an important food production area. Cheese from Olmsted Township and wine from Willoughby were consumed as far away as New Orleans. All the stuff being produced here was transported to areas that couldn't get enough of it—fruit and fruit products, and dairy products like cheeses. After the Civil War, this area was the leading fruit-producing area in the nation, and the leading wine-producing area, and known for stone fruits like cherries and peaches. Maple sugar cannot be overlooked either, although it has sort of dropped out of our culinary vocabulary. It used to be more important a long time ago.

Food writer Paris Wolfe Ferrante grew up appreciating the culinary wealth of rural Geauga County, including fresh produce sold from stands across the road and more.

> Imagine my surprise at age 13, when a friend poured maple-flavored corn syrup on my pancakes. Yuk! Why would anyone do that when they live so close to Chardon, Ohio, the maple capital of my childhood world? As a child, I didn't realize that Vermont owned the maple syrup title. I thought Ohio did. Northeast Ohio was a great place to source food. My parents visited an Amish butcher twice a year, picking up frozen white packages that added up to half a cow. I was under 10 when I walked through the cooler where sides of beef were aging. I can still picture all that meat hanging from hooks. It gave me the chills, and not because it was cold in there.

ON OUR PLATES:
Cleveland is known for foods such as pierogies, bratwurst, and mustard.

"In college, I was known as the pickle-packing momma."

Food memories from childhood warm our hearts or chill our bones. Food has an impact that's cultural, economic, nutritional, and social. Pat Bertman Mazoh's father founded Joe Bertman Foods, which today makes Bertman's Ball Park Mustard. She says, "My father started in business in 1925 as Bertman Pickle Company. In college, I was known as the pickle-packing momma. I claimed that pickles sent me to college. They were very good pickles. Dad made Polish dills."

Here are some examples of manufactured chow that put Cleveland on the food map.

BEEMAN'S PEPSIN GUM

Edwin Beeman began manufacturing his Beeman's Pepsin Gum in Cleveland at the Beeman Chemical Company in the 1890s. The company was sold to the American Chicle Company at the turn of the century.

DAN DEE PRETZEL & POTATO CHIP COMPANY

Originally located on Hough Avenue, the Dan Dee Pretzel & Potato Chip Company relocated to 2900 East 65th Street in the 1920s. The pretzel company's founders had moved to Cleveland from Pittsburgh in 1916, and potato chips were added to the product line a decade later. The company went through a few name changes before becoming the Dan Dee Pretzel & Potato Chip Company. As late as the 1940s, Dan Dee pretzels were still being twisted by hand; an experienced pretzel-twister could crank one out every two seconds.

> My grandmother came here from Lithuania at 15. My mother grew up on steak and baked potatoes, because my grandmother said, "No dumplings in America." She said she didn't come to this country to eat dumplings. My grandmother discovered doughnuts and potato chips here. She thought potato chips were just the best thing. The Dan Dee factory was not far from where she lived, and she could walk there and buy them fresh. – Lyn Byrd

Incidentally, while potato chips are said to have originated in Saratoga Springs, New York, one of the first potato-chip factories in the U.S. was started in Cleveland in 1895 by William Tappendon.

monaco's
meat sauce for
spaghetti
• heat and serve five

choice beef • mushrooms • tomato puree • onions
garlic • sugar • imported spices and seasonings,
contains no fillers, preservatives or coloring matter

coronet food products • cleveland • ohio

CHEF BOYARDEE

Nobody's spaghetti sauce is as good as your mom's, but for many Cleveland children, Chef Boyardee was their mom's spaghetti sauce. Chef Hector Boiardi (1897–1985) came to Cleveland in 1917. Chef Boiardi's Restaurant opened at 823 Prospect Avenue in 1931; the name was later changed to Chef Hector's in 1946, and the restaurant closed in 1967. Boiardi's Chef Boyardee became a well-known brand in Cleveland and around the country. Boiardi also had an interest in three other restaurants: Monaco's, Pierre's, and Town and Country. Chef Boyardee spaghetti was a serious favorite of many Cleveland kids.

"In elementary school, we went home for lunch," recalls Carol Lally Metz. "My dad made my favorite lunch, which was Chef Boyardee ravioli. He had an ingenious cooking system that cut down on pot washing. He'd take the lid off the can and put the can in boiling water. When the ravioli was heated through, he'd pour it onto the plates, empty and dry off the pan, and he was done."

THE MAN ON THE CAN: Chef Hector Boiardi (shown moving furniture with Frank Monaco) had an interest in several restaurants besides his own, Chef Hector's.

"He had an ingenious cooking system that cut down on pot washing."

**MAKING LOTS OF
BREAD: Laub Baking
Company on Lorain
Avenue was once Ohio's
biggest wholesale
bakery.**

LAUB BAKING COMPANY

Love that Laub's! Laub Baking Company at 4919 Lorain
Avenue was at one time Ohio's largest wholesale bakery. It
was founded in 1889 and remained open until the 1970s.
J. Spang Baking Comapny on Barber Avenue was a retail
baking company founded in 1894. It operated until 1958,
when it was sold to the Laub Baking Company.

ORLANDO BAKING COMPANY

The Orlando Baking Company established its roots here when part of the Orlando
family moved from Italy to Cleveland in 1904. Thus began the company's long experience in baking bread, including artisan breads.

LIFE SAVERS

Life Savers were developed in Cleveland by Clarence A. Crane, the chocolate
manufacturer and father of poet Hart Crane. In 1912, Crane's Peppermint Life
Savers were introduced. In 1913, Crane sold the trademark for $2,900 to two New
York businessmen.

ICE AGE: Stouffer's Frozen Foods were hot in 1954, but the company's shipping room on Woodland Avenue was way cool, at -25 degrees F.

PIERRE'S FRENCH ICE CREAM COMPANY

The Pierre's French Ice Cream Company started on East 82nd and Euclid in 1932. It moved to East 60th and Hough in 1960, where it shared a plant with the Royal Ice Cream Company. The latter acquired Pierre's and expanded its distribution. Then, in 1967, Harwill Ice Cream Company was brought into the fold.

STOUFFER FOODS

Stouffer Foods evolved out of a stand-up lunch counter in the Arcade in 1922, to restaurants, to prepared foods, to frozen meals. In 1953, a Woodland Avenue facility was opened to distribute its frozen foods.

FIZZY STUFF: we filled our glasses with Royal Crown Cola, Cotton Club Crème Soda, and other carbonated favorites.

COTTON CLUB

Cotton Club Bottling & Canning Company began making soft drinks in Cleveland in 1902. It relocated around town several times, until a new bottling plant was built in 1954 at 4922 East 49th Street in Cuyahoga Heights. That was also when the company began putting its products in cans as well as bottles. In 1963, the company bought Royal Crown Bottling Company and changed its name to Cotton Club Beverages.

Lilli Lief, who grew up in Shaker Heights, remembers drinking Cotton Club soft drinks. "We'd have Cotton Club at all of our family get-togethers—the cherry strawberry, and the crème soda."

DOUBLE EAGLE

The Double Eagle Bottling Company started brewing ginger beer in 1909 at 1838 St. Clair. During Prohibition, the company made carbonated ginger beer, and it remained in business until 1959.

Native Clevelander Joe Valencic recalls small bottles of Double Eagle's DEB Root Beer: "I wish I had one of their tin signs with the blonde debutante with a bottle of DEB Root Beer."

COCA-COLA TIDBITS: the "contour bottle" we all recognize arrived on the scene in 1916. In 1981, the Cleveland Coca-Cola Bottling Company celebrated its 50th anniversary.

LEISY BREWING COMPANY

Leisy Brewing Company, founded in 1873, was located at 3400 Vega on Cleveland's West Side. In the 1950s, it counted among its brands Leisy Light, Leisy Black Dallas (malt liquor), Mell-Gold, and Dortmunder. It ceased operations in 1959.

PILSENER BREWERY

Pilsener Brewery, founded in 1892, started on the corner of Clark Avenue and West 65th Street and made P.O.C. (the initials originally stood for Pilsener of Cleveland). In 1963, Pilsener's parent company sold the P.O.C. brand to the Duquesne Brewing Company. When Duquesne subsequently sold its brands to C. Schmidt & Sons in 1973, P.O.C. was back to being made in Cleveland until 1984.

> I had a brewery on my street. Red Cap, Old Timer's, and Black Label . . . just about everybody in the neighborhood drank those beers . . . And P.O.C. was a popular beer they had down at the ball games. – *Robert McAlpine*

STANDARD BREWING

Standard Brewing started up in 1904, at 5801 Train Avenue on the city's west side. Its brands included Erin Brew and Old Bohemian. The company was sold in 1961 to the F. M. Schaefer Brewing Company of New York. In 1964, Schaefer sold the brewery to C. Schmidt & Sons of Philadelphia. Schmidt relocated to the Carling Brewing plant in 1972.

In the 1950s, our locally made beers kind of went Hollywood with their promotional efforts and advertising. Clevelanders might have played a game back then called "match-the-national-celebrity-with-a-local-brew." If there had been such a game, these would have been the correct answers: Bob Hope (Pilsener P.O.C. ads); Basil Rathbone ("Leisy Premiere Theatre" host on TV); Lucille Ball (Carling Red Cap Ale ads). You'd get a bonus point for also mentioning Phil Silvers and Ethel Merman for appearing in Carling ads.

And speaking of popular culture, in the 1950s, "Hey Mabel, Black Label" was a popular ad slogan for beer. All that promotion must have paid off, too, because in 1965, more than 5.7 million barrels of Carling Beer were sold, and the brewery was one of the country's biggies.

BREW-LA-LA: beer was an integral part of Cleveland's past, associated with ball games, rocking good times, and good meals.

CARLING BREWING COMPANY

The Carling Brewing Company made its debut in 1933 at 9400 Quincy Avenue. It started as Brewing Corporation of America. James A. Bohannon, who had been president of Peerless Motor Car Company, converted the Peerless plant to a brewery. In 1944, the brewer also acquired the Tip Top and Forest City breweries. In 1954, it changed its name to the Carling Brewing Company. Its brands included Red Cap Ale and Black Label. It closed the Cleveland plant in 1971.

LOCAL WINERIES

In 1937, Anna and Nicholas Ferrante opened their winery in the Collinwood area, and in the 1970s, their sons Peter and Anthony built winemaking facilities at the family's vineyards in Harpersfield Township. In 1968, Markko Vineyard opened in Conneaut. But these were by no means the beginnings of wineries in Northeast Ohio.

Robert Louis Stevenson (1850–1894) described wine as "bottled poetry," so it shouldn't surprise us too much to hear that Henry Wadsworth Longfellow (1807–1882) waxed poetic about Ohio wines in his poem "Ode to Catawba Wine." Granted, both writers lived a long time ago, but back in 1860, Ohio was the nation's leading wine-producing state. After southern Ohio vineyards succumbed to disease, the Lake Erie Islands became Ohio's new vineyard area, and by 1900, there were dozens of wineries that flourished until Prohibition came along, beginning in 1919.

Food writer Paris Wolfe Ferrante recalls, "Local food introduced me to my husband. I was writing about the history of Ferrante Winery for a newspaper article. When the story was done, I went back to try the wine. Peter Ferrante (not the dad, the son) was working there and used free wine to flirt with me."

Clevelander Joe Valencic, who grew up in the North Collinwood neighborhood, talks about wineries in town, including one that was owned by his brother-in-law's cousins on St. Clair Avenue at East 61st Street. "Bozeglav Winery was bonded, producing its own wine from Geneva-grown grapes. I believe people could also bring in their own grapes and have them crushed or bottled."

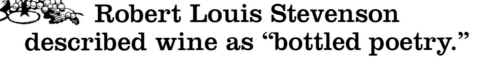

Robert Louis Stevenson described wine as "bottled poetry."

Cooking and Eating at Home

Imagine you are back in your mother's kitchen, lifting the lid off a pot bubbling on the stove. If you close your eyes and inhale, you might recall the aroma of fragrant sautéed greens, or simmering tomato sauce, or steamy chicken soup.

☞

HOME ON THE RANGE: home kitchens were the heart of the house, and new appliances such as stoves and refrigerators updated and upgraded the way we ate.

Whatever your heritage, those food memories have the power today to connect you with your own past. Perhaps your holiday memories are wrapped up with recollections of small children wearing pitted black olives on their fingers, or your grandmother presenting her famous-in-the-family sweet potato pie. Each family's kitchen culture is a blend of history and tradition. Collectively, these memories provide a snapshot of the distinctive flavor of Cleveland.

Through the Kitchen Door

Peek into any home kitchen and you get a glimpse of the inner workings of the family who cooks and eats there. Mealtimes connect us with our culture and kin, and the family kitchen is at the very core of that connection. Cleveland's kitchens of yesteryear were often a hub of activity.

What do you remember about your mother's kitchen? Perhaps you recall a white counter with gold flecks in it, an oilcloth covering on a drop-leaf table, a shiny chrome dinette set with red vinyl seats on the chairs, or a cozy breakfast nook with booths built into the wall.

Details may vary, but food remains a common denominator. It also carries cultural significance. Cookbooks from any era reflect not only the way we ate, but also the way we lived. More than anything, the family kitchen was—and still is—a state of mind.

Whether your family used its kitchen to cook, to reheat, or simply as a place to gather together and linger, it was an integral part of your childhood. Many of us recall our early food memories through a fond fog of nostalgia. In fact, cooking hot food during our cold winters steamed up a lot of windows, and made an impression on us.

You don't have to go out to have fond food memories. Native Clevelander Miriam Carey notes the special role of a family's kitchen.

In our kitchen everyone knew that the green Fiestaware bowl kept just over the cupboard next to the stove was for the express purpose of making fresh whipped cream. It was to be chilled, along with the whisks from the mixer, at least one hour before dinner and brought out only after the coffee was turned on so that the whipped cream would be as fresh, stiff, and cold as humanly possible.

The Chock Full o'Nuts coffee can next to the stove was there for draining fat . . . and everyone knew that the jar of Seaway Maraschino cherries in the refrigerator was never—ever—to be touched: It was a feat of physics that my father had engineered to hold the entire Frigidaire together.

Here's a peek into more Cleveland kitchens from bygone eras.

I had the job of emptying the water pan out of the icebox. The stove was a coal-cooking stove. You lifted the top off and put in a lump of coal. We baked in there—baked biscuits,

Feature of Ideal Spring Party
(See recipe for Peach Down Side Up Cake)

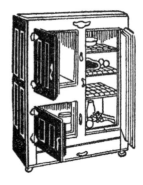

Recipes and Menus Developed in the Sealtest Laboratory Kitchen, Radio City, New York

CAULIFLOWER POWER: in the 1930s, cooking information from food or appliance companies advised home cooks on how to make the most of their food dollar.

cake, and cornbread—and I don't understand how it kept the temperature. I still don't like that yellow cornmeal bread. – *Robert McAlpine, Cleveland (Near East Side)*

I remember a big table in the middle of the room where food was prepared. My mother was a baker. Not a professional, but she baked cakes and pies from scratch. And I remember the ice-boxes. My grandmother had one until the 1950s. I remember the ice people coming in, and my grandmother and mother working hard at the table. – *Joe Terebieniec, Cleveland (West 25th Street/Clark Avenue)*

We couldn't play outside because my grandmother had to be able to see us. She cooked a lot, so we played in the kitchen. She cooked soul food, and we had hot tea with every meal. In the morning, my grandmother would get up and put the teakettle on the table. She liked to bake. Teacakes were our treat. That was her specialty. – *Dorothy Bell, Cleveland (East Side)*

Seldom (thankfully) used for cooking, my mother's kitchen was a wonderland of Ohio Blue Tips, a cherry table with drop leafs, and all sorts of bottles, jars, and containers for our ongoing science and art adventures. These included brewing a primitive precursor to Play-Doh (quite yummy) and making rock candy (not so yummy).

The heat of the burners on our porcelain-finished gas Roper (with clock but sans pilot lights) revealed our secret messages written in lemon juice. On the windowsill, crystal islands grew on lumps of coal that were snatched from the railroad tracks behind our house and doused in a sea of laundry bluing filling a pie tin. And there was so much more—papier-mâché animals, vinegar-and-baking-soda-powered tinfoil speed boats, and fuzzy little lumps of sprouts that some marketing guru would name "Chia Pets" decades later.

"Are you kids hungry?" my mom liked to say. "Let's go out and get something to eat." – *George Ghetia, Lakewood*

"I remember the ice people coming in."

We had a Formica kitchen set, the original set with wooden chairs and a ceramic-bonded-to-metal top. The base and legs of the kitchen table were wooden. We still have that set in the basement. There were frilly curtains on the windows, a half window over the sink, and a window on the back door with matching curtains. In a Slovenian kitchen you had a splash cloth, either behind the sink or behind the stove so that grease didn't splash on your wall. It was an embroidered cotton cloth that you attached to the wall somehow. You could buy them that way, but more often than not people got them from Slovenia or Germany or Hungary, with a motto—slogans about a mother's love or a religious thing—and some bucolic scene. Then you embroidered it. We had three or four that my mother made. About 15 years ago the Slovenian American National Art Guild came out with a book on splasher cloths.
– *Joe Valencic, Cleveland (North Collinwood/Beachland)*

My mother's kitchen was filled with canned goods—mostly Campbell's Soup. For lunch, we had Chef Boyardee Spaghetti, macaroni and cheese, baloney sandwiches, or cheese sandwiches. – *Dennis King, Rocky River*

My mother's kitchen was small. And because there were so many of us, my father built a triangular table that went into the corner, with two booths on the walls so they could fit all the kids in. We tried to eat together. My mother worked, and she left us instructions. She prepared the food, and we'd reheat it. Everybody would have to

KITCHEN SNAPSHOT:
Fundamental in the '50s

On our shelves: This is the era when can openers were king. Poppy Cannon's *The Can-Opener Cookbook* was published in 1952, and four years later, electric can openers went on the market.

Shopping habits: By 1952, the average supermarket in the U.S. stocked 4,000 items.

Hot and cold: Electric frying pans made the scene in 1953, and so did frozen Swanson TV Dinners. Back when TV sets had legs, eating in front of the tube was cool. By 1959, you could buy a Presto Fry Pan for $16.95 on sale at the May Company.

CAN DO: canned ethnic food products such as LaChoy noodles (started by a Detroit grocer) and spaghetti sauce expanded the culinary repertoire of Cleveland home cooks.

KITCHEN SNAPSHOT:
Standard in the '60s

As baby boomers became teens in this decade, their eating habits changed. People tuned in to cooking shows to get ideas for elegant home entertaining. French food was fine, and we took to quiche and fondue in a big way.

On our shelves: Wonder Bread was building strong bodies 12 ways, Kraft Barbecue Sauce was introduced, Tang instant orange juice (introduced in 1958) went into space, and Pop Tarts made the scene. Cold Duck was a hip drink, and spray cheese was all the rage.

Shopping habits: By the middle of the decade, the average supermarket stocked about 8,000 items. Approximately 75 percent of supermarkets were issuing trading stamps that allowed shoppers who collected them to earn premiums. We liked beef, but many people made Friday night's dinner a fish dinner. Plastic milk jugs were introduced in 1964.

Hot and cold: Teflon-coated cookware made mealtime cleanup easier, and the Salton Hotray was a hip and happening appliance to keep those dips and casseroles warm.

help. She cooked on Wednesdays and Sundays, because my father was a dentist and those were his days off. – *Jodi Kanter, Lyndhurst*

Our kitchen was the heart of our home. The kitchen table was where we ate, talked, played cards, and visited. Our kitchen was well equipped for feeding a family of seven—Mom, Dad, and five kids. We had a basic inventory of versatile pots, pans, and baking supplies. We had a deep-fryer for french fries and frozen fish and shrimp. We had a grinder and large slicer, which enabled us to maximize the use of leftovers. Ham and roast beef were sliced or ground for sandwiches for school days. Mom was a great baker. She would make bread and rolls, chocolate chip cookies, brownies, and cakes all from scratch. Her pie crust was outstanding."
– *Eileen Murray, North Olmsted*

Mom's narrow hallway of a kitchen, suited up with brown appliances, sans dishwasher or microwave, was a powerhouse. We cranked a cherry pitter, prepping sour cherries to be frozen for pies throughout the winter. Store-bought pie was unthinkable.

At dawn in midsummer my mom drove 15 miles south to Middlefield for fresh-picked peaches. Then, we'd sweat all day in an un-airconditioned and breezeless kitchen, slipping off skins and capturing their sunset richness before the sugars would fade.

Not long after, Mom would arrange with another farmer to get just-picked cucumbers for homemade pickles. If the cukes sat overnight, they'd be too soft for great pickles. We'd get them in a crock and make sure someone would babysit them if we went away for a weekend. – *Paris Wolfe Ferrante, Hambden Township*

My mother's kitchen was a sweltering, dizzying array of heat, smells, and tastes. From whole chickens stewing in shiny steel pots along with chopped-up celery, carrots, and the foam of fat that rose to the top, homemade noodles from an aunt three streets away, and fist-sized bay leaves, to pork or lamb roasting in the oven. In the winter, the windows would fog up from the steam.
– *Milenko Budimir, Cleveland (Broadway and East 65th, Union Avenue,)*

A GUIDE TO

ROYAL SUCCESS IN BAKING

ROYAL BAKING POWDER

BY THE BOOK: makers of baking powder, gelatin, sugar, and chocolate all produced free recipe pamphlets to encourage home cooks to broaden their horizons.

FISH PHASE

While some of us were happy with fish sticks, other Clevelanders took advantage of the bounty of our regional waters. In 1954, 75 million pounds of commercial fish were pulled out of Lake Erie. That's a lot of fish, and we had many types from which to choose.

In 1968 at the Second Annual Sun Papers Big Fish Contest (open to residents of the West Side suburbs and Cleveland's West Park neighborhood), eligible species of fish caught in Ohio included largemouth and smallmouth bass, rock bass, white bass, bluegill, crappie, carp, perch, walleye, northern pike, muskellunge, rainbow trout, channel catfish, bullhead, sheephead, and smelt. While they might not be so quick to share the catch, Clevelanders are always willing to share their fond fishing memories.

> I love fishing. I caught perch, bluegill, and crappies. I can remember catching bluegill in the river before the river got oily. They've got walleye in it now, good fish. But that sheephead—everybody ate it. I didn't even like it. It's also called drum. The meat is coarse. I like the white bass that comes out of the lake. When I cook it, I can only get one side of that lake perch crispy. – *Robert McAlpine*

> The man next door to us was a commercial Lake Erie fisherman, so he'd bring fish to us. We had fresh fish, because he went fishing every day."
> – *Mary Ghetia, Cleveland (West 45th and Tillman Avenue)*

> I fished off Bradstreet's Landing pier when I was a kid. Then, I went out on a boat with friends. We'd cook them up in my friend Pat's backyard over a grill in a big frying pan. Chef Pat did the cooking. We'd sit back there all night and drink beer and eat perch. We still go out on a boat, get perch, and cook them up there right away. There's nothing better than fresh Lake Erie perch. It's the best fish there is.
> – *Dennis King*

> It wasn't until I was grown up and writing about food that it finally occurred to me that not everyone ate Lake Erie perch and walleye. I was shocked when people asked me what bluegill tasted like. We pulled them from ponds and ate them for dinner. They rival the best Lake Erie perch. – *Paris Wolfe Ferrante*

KITCHEN SNAPSHOT:
Standard in the '70s and Beyond

With the advent of Nouvelle Cuisine, we moved from the heavier style of classic French cooking to the lighter, brighter flavors of reduced sauces made without thickeners, and fresh vegetables cooked to the tender-crisp stage. We hosted and attended sophisticated wine and cheese parties. Natural foods gained a stronghold, and granola and carob were new words in our culinary vocabulary.

On our shelves: Chicken was becoming chic, carbonated drink sales had just overtaken coffee sales, and healthful food was on the rise.

Shopping habits: Between 5,000 and 10,000 food co-ops sprang up in the 1970s. Cleveland's Food Co-Op was already established at 11702 Euclid Avenue in University Circle.

Hot and cold: Rival Manufacturing Company introduced the Crock-Pot in a variety of trendy appliance colors, including flaming bright orange, coppery brown, harvest gold, and cool avocado green. Serious cooks pined for food processors.

"I was shocked when people asked me what bluegill tasted like."

HOLIDAY ON ICE

1953: The Swanson TV Dinner (turkey, stuffing, peas, potatoes) offered Thanksgiving-style fare, served up on a sectioned aluminum tray reminiscent of the compartmentalized airline meal trays. The cost was 98 cents.

THE COOKING CONNECTION: in the 1950s, slogans like "The Burner with a Brain" spurred us on to buy bigger and better ranges.

Some folks bought their seafood, of course. Patrick Miller of Aurora remembers his parents buying live lobsters in the 1970s. "They had a steamer and steamed them. I was a kid and it freaked me out. At first it was traumatic, but I ate it. All of it."

Chilling Out and Heating Up

To say people weren't trendsetters way back when would be a mistake. It's just that what was new and hip then (waffle irons, refrigerators, electric ranges) is now standard equipment. Women sent away for recipe brochures from makers of refrigerators, as well as from utility companies, and a host of food manufacturers.

"Now you're cooking with gas" was a slogan that many Clevelanders adopted as part of popular speech, meaning "Now you're catching on." Converting from iceboxes to refrigerators, or from old-fashioned stoves to gas or electric cooking, was no breeze for many Cleveland households. Such upgrades often required a familiarization period, and the utility companies were there to help. They offered consumers booklets and instruction manuals that were designed to give no-nonsense

advice to home cooks, experienced and inexperienced alike. The utility companies also provided services to commercial food-service customers. Getting kitchen appliances was a big deal.

> We had a 1940 General Electric refrigerator that served us well until about 1980. When we gave it away, it still worked. My family lived around East 64th and St. Clair then, and my mother was the first in her circle of friends to buy a refrigerator. Everybody razzed my father no end—why would they spend so much money just to cool a quart of milk and a stick of butter? My mother was sick of stuff spoiling. It liberated her as a homemaker. You shopped every day, at mom-and-pop stores, because you didn't have a refrigerator. She could shop less. Within months, everybody who had poked fun got a refrigerator. Ours had rounded edges, a long handle you pulled towards you, and shiny chrome grills or racks. – *Joe Valencic*

> We didn't have a refrigerator until 1938. The iceman would come and have a huge piece of thick leather over his shoulder, and take a big pick to get a 25-pound piece of ice. He'd bring it in and it would last a week. People had to go the grocery store every day. – *Mary Ghetia*

> My mother-in-law has probably made two million cookies in her lifetime. Italian biscotti. She makes them for any occasion—for funerals or for parties. She goes through tons of flour and sugar every year. She buys 100-pound bags. She used to have a very old oven; she propped a chair against the door to keep it closed, and guessed at the heat. Nobody in the family has learned how to make those cookies. – *Jim Kovach, Cleveland*

The Cleveland Electric Illuminating Company produced guides such as "Maple Syrup and Maple Sugar: 12 Delicious Ways to Use Them." Besides providing recipes, the guide also promised to demonstrate how "the electric range and the electric refrigerator will prove their superior advantages."

Therese Hummer, who served as commercial food-service representative for the Illuminating Company from 1971 to 1991, promoted the use of electric cooking equipment by publicizing its advantages, including cleanliness, safety, and accuracy of temperature. "We dealt with anybody who used commercial cooking equipment," she explains.

Fuel use was an important concern during the years of World War II, and later it took on importance again during the energy crisis in the early 1970s. The wartime rationing and shortages of the 1940s were addressed in food writer M. F. K. Fisher's classic book of essays, *How to Cook a Wolf.* There's a Cleveland connection, too. After the book was first published in 1942, a later edition was

LONG-RANGE PLANS: pamphlets promoting particular ingredients and cooking techniques also educated consumers about the advantages of new appliances.

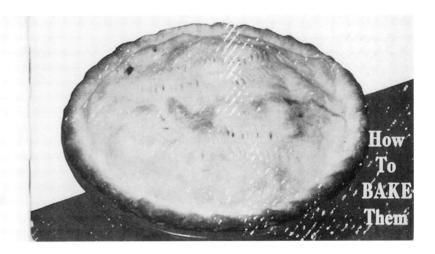

**COOKING & CHILLING:
a refrigerator is to
salads what a stove is to
pies. Home cooks sent
away for free cookbooks
to learn why**

published by World Publishing Company in Cleveland in 1944. In it, Fisher writes, "Women who never thought one way or another about such things before are going to find that fuel and light, even if they have enough money to pay for them, may be scarce and impossible to hoard, and after the first sense of irritation will learn to cook well and intelligently and economically with very little gas or electricity."

The East Ohio Gas Company's Home Service Department published booklets such as a cooking and baking guide titled "Cookies: How to Make Them" and a pie-making guide titled "How to Bake Them." The pie guide suggested crust alternatives such as cornflakes or zwieback. The company worked with commercial customers as well as consumers. Gary Grabowski, who operated Miracles restaurant in Tremont, explains, "East Ohio Gas had a department that specifically catered to restaurants. What they did was promote restaurant-type appliances, gas appliances. They also came in and calibrated your stove."

Cleveland cooks also sent away for free cooking pamphlets such as "The Frigidaire Salad Book" that offered suggestions for creating chilled salads. These included a quivering concoction called Perfection Salad, made with gelatin, sugar, cabbage, celery, pimentos, and green peppers. The idea was that you needed the refrigerator to make the recipes.

Food and Fellowship

As Mark Lewine, professor of anthropology and urban studies at Cuyahoga Community College, says, "Working with others preparing foods for a large group is, in the deepest sense, a form of fellowship. People relax, and share very powerful connections." Many locals have fond memories that blend food and fellowship.

The food memories of Clevelander Mary E. Weems fit into this category:

> When I think about food and childhood, only one event comes to mind, our annual Fourth of July family reunion picnic. No one knows "exactly" when it started, but my Auntie Edna, who will be 90 in 2004, says she can't remember a time when we didn't have it. When I think food, I think family. As time continues to do its marathon, and different faces at our picnics change from young to old, I'm reminded of how much the look, smell, and flavor of food is woven into my family tree.

Meanwhile, other Northeast Ohioans link food memories with fellowship in a variety of settings.

> I remember breakfast on Easter, after the sunrise service at Christ the King Lutheran Church—scrambled eggs, toast, and orange juice. – *Susanne Apple, Macedonia*

> At Euclid Beach Park, we'd have the temple picnic. All the families from the temple would meet there. – *Lilli Lief, Shaker Heights*

> I'm a church man. That's where I got most of my entertainment—at church. We'd have Sunday dinner quite often at church, and cookouts in the summertime. – *Casey Claytor, Cleveland*

> I remember the ladies making pierogies in the kitchen and selling them for church functions because so many people wanted them. – *Joe Terebieniec*

> The Holy Name Society had breakfasts at the Hollenden once or twice a year. The fathers and sons were in suits, and some sportscaster or semiretired jock would give a speech. Those were big events. They served standard breakfast stuff, but it was my first time in a fancy downtown hotel. If you hadn't been in one, they seemed like palaces. – *Bob Krummert*

"I didn't think white folks barbecued."

RIB-IT: over the years, rib cooking has been elevated to an art. At a National Rib Cook-Off held in the 1980s, winners included Pacer's of Euclid, Tony Roma's (Cleveland), and Brassy's (Brunswick).

FOOD AT FAIRS AND FESTIVALS

When my husband and I were dating, we went to the Hessler Street Fair and bought giant cups of freshly made lemonade, made by the medical students. It was the best lemonade I've ever had—cold, sweet, and so tart that your salivary glands would go into overload. – Pat Fernberg

Paris Wolfe Ferrante has sweet food festival memories too. "The Maple Festival was the highlight of my spring. It's celebrated the weekend after Easter. When Easter fell in March, we needed mittens and parkas and hot chocolate. When Easter was in late April, it was sunny and warm, and you couldn't drink enough old-fashioned lemonade. When I was a child, it was about the kiddie rides and maple stirs. As a teen, it was about boys, thrill rides, and maple candy. Now that I have children, it's again about the kiddie rides and maple cotton candy."

We were one of the first groups to go down and get in the rib burn-offs. Then when they went nationwide, the guys with big money pushed us out of the way. Just about all the black stores would participate. I didn't think white folks barbecued. We got a great big old wash pan and put the coals in that, and wires going over the top. Every other house in the neighborhood sold barbecue. And I'm talking about some barbecue. You could smell it from 55th Street all the way downtown. – Robert McAlpine

I've been to the Rib Burn-Off quite a few times. The ribs are the best on the last day, because they're cheaper. After a bad weekend, they'd be cheaper, too. – Dennis King

Taste Yesterday Today

A Blast from Our Culinary Past

You can still shop the way your grandparents did at the West Side Market, and you can order eggs and coffee at a number of area diners. Clevelanders may lament the closing of Alesci's in North Olmsted, but Alesci's of South Euclid continues to serve customers, as it has since 1956. The whimsical interior of Malley's in Lakewood has changed, but the ice-cream parlor recalled in these pages still exists. And that's not all. Here are some sources to help you recapture an elusive bit of your own culinary past.

RELIVING THE EUCLID BEACH EXPERIENCE

Humphrey Kisses and Popcorn Balls are available at area stores, including Marc's, Giant Eagle, and Heinen's. And the style of frozen custard you remember is available at East Coast Custard.

The Humphrey Company
20810 Miles Pkwy.
Warrensville Hts., OH 44124
(216) 662-6629
www.humphreycompany.com

East Coast Original Frozen Custard
1257 Pearl Rd. in Brunswick
810 East 222nd St. in Euclid
18900 Lorain Rd. in Fairview Park
5618 Mayfield Rd. in Lyndhurst
7577 Mentor Ave. in Mentor
6240 Pearl Rd. in Parma Hts.
www.eastcoastcustard.com

RECAPTURING THE FLAVOR OF HOUGH BAKERY

You can order cakes and some other specialties you might recall from Hough Bakery (large orders only) at Archie's Lakeshore Bakery. It's operated by Archie Garner, who was formerly the head baker in Hough Bakery's catering department. Sheet cakes are available in a quarter-sheet size (serves 15–20), half-sheet (serves up to 50), and a full-sheet size that serves up to 100 people. Archie's Lakeshore Bakery is closed on Sundays and Mondays.

Archie's Lakeshore Bakery
14906 Lake Shore Blvd.
Cleveland, OH
(216) 481-4188

REMEMBERING LUCY'S

The bakery so many people remember on Buckeye Road is now owned by Michael Feigenbaum, who inherited some of Lucy's recipes.

Lucy's Sweet Surrender
12516 Buckeye Rd.
Cleveland, OH 44120
(216) 752-0828

RECALLING THE FROSTY BAR AT HIGBEE'S

Weber's opened in 1931, and its frosted malt is said to have been the inspiration for the Frosty Bar specialty available at Higbee's and the May Company. You can still taste that flavor today in Weber's frosted-malt-flavor premium custard.

Weber's Premium Custard & Ice Cream
20230 Lorain Rd.
Fairview Park, OH 44126
(440) 331-0004
www.weberscustard.com

BIG BOY SAUCE

Manners Big Boy may be gone, but Frisch's Big Boy is still distributing Frisch's Big Boy Tartar Sauce. It's made by the Food Specialties Company in Cincinnati. You can order a case of four pint bottles for $16.50. The price includes shipping.

Food Specialties Company
12 E. Sunnybrook Dr.
Cincinnati, OH 45237
(513) 761-1242
www.frischs.com

RETRO CANDY

You'll find Sky Bars, wax lips, Sen-Sen, and more. And while you won't get the thrill of that truck pulling up to the curb in front of your house, Charles Chips are available here too.

B.A. Sweetie Candy Company
5138 Mayfield Rd.
Lyndhurst, OH
(440) 605-0817

MUSTARD MEMORIES

As Michael Symon notes, "I think it's completely unique to this area that we have our own mustards. I've actually been to stadiums in other cities that have mustard from Cleveland." These are the tastes you associate with sporting events. "We're known for some of the best mustard produced for mass consumption," says Mark Lewine.

Original Bertman's Ball Park Mustard
Joe Bertman Foods
P.O. Box 6562
Cleveland, OH 44101
(800) 749-4460
Available at Heinen's, Marc's, Giant Eagle

The Authentic Stadium Mustard
Davis Food Company
1230 Bonnie Ln.
Mayfield Hts., OH 44124
(440) 461-2885
www.stadiummustard.com
Available at Heinen's, Marc's, Tops, Giant Eagle

RESTAURANT SPECIALTIES THAT LIVE ON

Years ago, one of the favorites on Stouffer's restaurant menu was macaroni and cheese. And of course you can still buy it, as well as other frozen entrees popularized at the restaurant, at area supermarkets.

Similarly, Chef Hector Boiardi created pasta for posterity. His restaurant is gone but today we can still buy Chef Boyardee Ravioli, and other products are available at area supermarkets.

If you're pining for the Brown Sauce you used to order on your pasta at the New York Spaghetti House, you'll be happy to learn that frozen versions of three of the sauces—Brown, Marinara, and Romana—are available at area Heinen's stores.

HIGBEE'S SILVER GRILLE

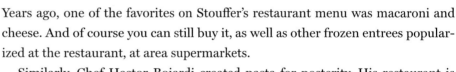

It's not really back, but it has been opened for private parties. "I got a courtesy walk-through from the Tower City people," says Jim McConnell, the restaurant's last food-service director. "I'm glad to see Tower City sank in as much money as they did to redo it. The kitchen is gone—there's only a rewarming kitchen—but the dining room is done in the original colors."

Acknowledgments

I am grateful to the following people who generously shared their memories, their resources, their expertise and, above all, their enthusiasm to help bring this book to fruition. While I couldn't include all of their food memories in detail, their contributions nevertheless helped bring the past into yummy focus: Susanne Apple, Luanne Bole-Becker, Bob Becker, Dorothy Bell, Jean D. Bellamy, John S. Bellamy II, Sheila Bellamy, Candace Bohn, Salwa Boukair, Milenko Budimir, Laura Budny, Lyn Byrd, Miriam Carey, James "Casey" Claytor, Anna Chenin, Patricia Demski, Sam DeGaetano, Jan DeLucia, David Farkas, Pat Fernberg, Paris Wolfe Ferrante, Janet Beighle French, George A. Ghetia, Mary V. Ghetia, Gary Grabowski, Rita M. Grabowski, Willy Herzberger, Therese Hummer, Aaron Jacobson, Jodi Kanter, Dennis King, Jim Kovach, Bob Krummert, Anne Kwait, Jane Lassar, John Lawn, Mark Lewine, Ph.D., Lilli Lief, Rita Pavny Lockman, John Long, Carl LoPresti, Larisa Lucaci, Joann Macias, Tony Macias, Pat Bertman Mazoh, Robert McAlpine, Jim McConnell, Sali A. McSherry, Carol Lally Metz, Stephen G. Michaelides, Patrick Miller, Eileen Murray, Glen Nekvasil, Don Odiorne, Janice Orr, Laurie Orr, Karen Perry, Herman Pirchner, Steve Presser, Don Raith, Christopher Roberto, Linda Goodman Robiner, Marie DeLuca Sandru, Michael Sanson, Anita Simon, Marge Skof, Katie Smith, Marie Smith, Michael Symon, Laura Taxel, Joe Terebieniec, Doris Urbansky, Tom Urbansky, Joe Valencic, Mary E. Weems, Helen Weinberger, Angela Wilkes, Claire A. Wirt, and Ellie Yanky. Finally, I am especially indebted to my husband, Stephen Paul Bellamy, for his cheerful assistance at every step along the way.

Sources

American Restaurant Magazine 14, no. 4 (April 1931): 49.

Beard, James. *Beard on Bread.* New York: Alfred A. Knopf, 1974.

Bower, Anne L., ed. *Recipes for Reading: Community Cookbooks, Stories, Histories.* Amherst: University of Massachusetts Press, 1997.

Bundy, Beverly. *The Century in Food.* Portland, Ore.: Collectors Press, 2002.

Bush, Leo O., Edward C. Chukayne, Russell Allon Hehr, and Richard F. Hershey. *Euclid Beach Park: A Second Look.* Mentor, Oh.: Amusement Park Books, 1979.

———. *Euclid Beach Park is Closed for the Season.* Fairview Park, Oh.: Amusement Park Books, 1977.

Butko, Brian. *Klondikes, Chipped Ham & Skyscraper Cones: The Story of Isaly's.* Mechanicsburg, Pa.: Stackpole Books, 2001.

Chase's Calendar of Events 2003. Chicago: Contemporary Books, 2003.

Deluca, Michael, and Stephen Michaelides. *Dining In—Cleveland.* Mercer Island, Wash.: Peanut Butter Publishing, 1982.

Elkort, Martin. *The Secret Life of Food.* Los Angeles: Jeremy P. Tarcher, 1991.

Engel, Allison, and Margaret Engel. *Food Finds: America's Best Local Foods and the People Who Produce Them.* New York: Quill, 2000.

Fisher, M. F. K. *How to Cook a Wolf.* Cleveland: World Publishing, 1944.

French, Janet Beighle. "Dining Out." *The Plain Dealer Magazine,* Dec. 1, 1991.

Full Face. The Gruber Hollenden Foundation: Cleveland, 1954.

Herbst, Sharon Tyler. *The New Food Lover's Companion.* Hauppauge, N.Y.: Barron's, 2001.

Hilton, Conrad N. *The Hilton International Cookbook.* Englewood Cliffs, N.J.: Prentice Hall, 1960.

Hines, Duncan. *Duncan Hines' Food Odyssey.* New York: Thomas Y. Crowell, 1955.

Hoover, Earl R. *Cradle of Greatness.* Cleveland: Shaker Savings Association, 1977.

Karberg, Richard E., with Judith Karberg and Jane Hazen. *The Higbee Company and the Silver Grille.* Cleveland: Cleveland Landmarks Press, 2001.

———. *The Silver Grille: Memories and Recipes.* Cleveland: Cleveland Landmarks Press, 2000.

Labensky, Steven, Gaye G. Ingram, and Sarah R. Labensky. *Webster's New World Dictionary of Culinary Arts.* Upper Saddle River, N.J.: Prentice Hall, 1997.

Lovegren, Sylvia. *Fashionable Food.* New York: Macmillan, 1995.

Miller, Carl H. *Breweries of Cleveland.* Cleveland: Schnitzelbank Press, 1998.

Nulmoor, H. C. "The Forums Do It Again." *The American Restaurant Magazine* 14, no. 8 (August 1931): 48–49.

The Packer: A Century of Produce, 1893–1993. Lincolnshire, Ill.: Vance Publishing, 1993.

Rozin, Elizabeth. *Ethnic Cuisine.* New York: Penguin Books, 1992.

Schremp, Gerry. *Kitchen Culture.* New York: Pharos Books, 1991.

Strasser, Susan. *Never Done.* New York: Pantheon, 1982.

Taxel, Laura. *Cleveland Ethnic Eats,* 2003 ed. Cleveland: Gray & Company, Publishers, 2002.

Tennyson, Jeffrey. *Hamburger Heaven.* New York: Hyperion, 1993.

Trader Vic's Book of Food and Drink. Garden City, N.Y.: Doubleday, 1946.

Trager, James. *The Food Chronology.* New York: Henry Holt & Co., 1995.

Urdang, Laurence, ed. *The Timetables of American History.* New York: Simon & Schuster, 1996.

Van Tassel, David D., and John J. Grabowski, eds. *The Encyclopedia of Cleveland History.* Bloomington: Indiana University Press, 1987.

Wilson, Terry P. *The Cart That Changed the World.* Norman, Okla.: University of Oklahoma Press, 1978.

Young-Witzel, Gyvel, and Michael Karl Witzel. *Soda Pop!* Stillwater, Minn.: Town Square Books, 1998.

Photo Credits

Photos courtesy of:
p. 5, Steve Presser
p. 7, Candance Bohn
p. 8, Candance Bohn
p. 10, CSU*
p. 11, top right, Sheila Bellamy; bottom left, John Stark Bellamy, II; bottom left, author
p. 12, top right, Herman Pirchner; bottom right, author
p. 13 Candance Bohn
p. 14, top and middle right, Candance Bohn; bottom right, Doris Urbansky
p. 15, Candance Bohn
p. 16, bottom center, CSU; bottom right, Candace Bohn; top right, Willy Herzberger
p. 17, top, CSU; bottom, Candance Bohn; bottom left, John Stark Bellamy, II
p. 18, top, CSU; bottom, Candance Bohn
p. 19, top left, Candance Bohn; bottom, CSU
p. 20, CSU
p. 21, CSU
p. 22, CSU
p. 23 top left, Willy Herzberger; bottom left, CSU; right, Candance Bohn
p. 24, top left, Sheila Bellamy; right, CSU
p. 25, CSU; bottom left, author
p. 26, CSU
p. 27, Candance Bohn
p. 28, Candance Bohn
p. 29, CSU
p. 30, top right, Janet French; bottom, CSU
p. 31, Candace Bohn
p. 32, top right, John Stark Bellamy, II; bottom right, CSU
p. 33, CSU
p. 34, CSU, bottom right, Candance Bohn
p. 35, Candance Bohn
p. 36, George A. Ghetia
p. 37, CSU
p. 40, top, CSU; middle right, Candance Bohn
p. 41, Candance Bohn
p. 42, CSU
p. 43, CSU
p. 44, top right, Janet Beighle French; bottom right, John Stark Bellamy, II
p. 45, top left, author; bottom left, CSU
p. 46, top, Candance Bohn; bottom, CSU
p. 47, Willy Herzberger
p. 48, CSU
p. 49, top right, Candance Bohn; bottom, CSU
p. 51 top, Herman Pirchner; middle left, Candance Bohn
p. 52, CSU
p. 53, CSU
p. 54, CSU
p. 55, CSU

p. 56, CSU
p. 57, CSU
p. 58, Rita Pavny Lockman
p. 60, top, Candance Bohn; bottom, author and John Stark Bellamy, II
p. 61, CSU
p. 62, top right, Candance Bohn; bottom left, author
p. 63, CSU
p. 64, top, author; bottom, Candance Bohn
p. 65, CSU
p. 66, top right, Candance Bohn; bottom, Douglas C. Orr
p. 67, Candance Bohn
p. 68, CSU
p. 69, CSU
p. 70, top and bottom right, Candance Bohn; middle right, author
p. 71, top, Salwa Boukair; middle left, Candace Bohn
p. 72, CSU
p. 74, top right, Dairy Queen; bottom right, Candance Bohn
p. 76, Candance Bohn
p. 77, Candance Bohn
p. 78, top left, CSU; bottom right, Steve Presser
p. 79, CSU
p. 80, top left, CSU; right, Steve Presser
p. 82, top right, Steve Presser; bottom right, Candance Bohn
p. 83, top, CSU; bottom, Candance Bohn
p. 84, CSU
p. 85, Candance Bohn
p. 86, author
p. 88, top, CSU; middle left, Willy Herzberger
p. 89, top, CSU; middle left and right, Candance Bohn
p. 90, CSU
p. 91 top left, John Stark Bellamy, II; bottom left, CSU
p. 92, top left, Candance Bohn; bottom left, private collector; bottom right, author
p. 94, CSU
p. 96, author
p. 97, author
p. 98, bottom left, CSU; bottom right, author
p. 99, author
p. 101, author
p. 102, author
p. 103, left, author; right, Pat Fernberg
p. 105, Restaurant Hospitality
p. 106, author
p. 107, Steve Presser
p. 108, author
p. 109, author

* CSU - Cleveland Press Collection, Cleveland State University Archives